TOWARDS THE CONVERSION OF ENGLAND

TOWARDS THE
CONVERSION OF ENGLAND

Being the
REPORT OF A COMMISSION
ON EVANGELISM APPOINTED
BY THE ARCHBISHOPS OF
CANTERBURY AND YORK
PURSUANT TO A RESOLUTION
OF THE CHURCH ASSEMBLY
PASSED AT THE SUMMER
SESSION, 1943.

1945

Published by
THE PRESS AND PUBLICATIONS BOARD OF THE
CHURCH ASSEMBLY, 2 GREAT PETER STREET.
WESTMINSTER, S.W.1.

TERMS OF REFERENCE

"That the Assembly, recognising the urgent necessity for definite action, requests the Archbishops to appoint a Commission under Standing Order XVII to survey the whole problem of modern evangelism with special reference to the spiritual needs and prevailing intellectual outlook of the non-worshipping members of the community, and to report on the organization and methods by which such needs can most effectively be met."

(June 23, 1943)

MEMBERS

The Bishop of Rochester (*Chairman*)
Capt. L. W. Chidzey, C.A. (*Secretary*)

The Bishop of Chelmsford
The Bishop of Newcastle[1]
The Bishop of Southampton
The Bishop of Whitby
The Provost of Leicester
Mrs. H. Birch-Reynardson
Canon T. Bloomer
Canon G. W. Briggs
Mr. George Bromby
Miss E. A. M. Callister
Canon P. C. A. Carnegy
Miss Helena Charles
Canon C. R. Claxton
Lady Cynthia Colville
Fl.-Lt. J. H. Cordle
Captain R. G. Coulson
The Rev. R. H. de Pemberton
Lord Elton
Miss Lilias Graham[2]
Sir Arthur Griffith-Boscawen
The Rev. St. J. B. Groser
The Rev. H. G. Herklots
Miss Bridget Hill
Preb. H. W. Hinde

Canon Trevor J. Jones
Miss E. C. Knight-Bruce
Canon C. H. Lambert
Miss K. M. Lloyd
Canon R. B. Lloyd
The Rev. Howard G. Marshall
The Rev. C. B. Mortlock
The Rev. N. C. S. Motley
Miss Agatha Norman
Lt.-Col. H. L. Oldham
Mr. John B. Peile
Mrs. R. Prideaux
The Rev. A. S. Reeve
The Rev. W. S. A. Robertson
Mrs. Rose
The Rev. A. Mervyn Stockwood
Canon J. E. Swann
The Rev. E. K. Talbot
The Rev. H. H. Treacher
Miss Sibyl Thesiger
The Rev. Oliver S. Tomkins
Preb. J. W. Welch
The Rev. J. C. Winslow
Mr. Ernest T. Williams

---

[1] Resigned on leaving for Burma to visit H.M. Forces.
[2] Resigned on leaving England on War Service.

"*If we have to choose between making men Christian and making the social order more Christian, we must choose the former. But there is no such antithesis.*" WILLIAM TEMPLE.

FOREWORD

YOUR Commission was appointed by the Archbishops shortly after the November Session of the Church Assembly, 1943. It held its inaugural meeting on 18th February, 1944, in the Jerusalem Chamber, Westminster Abbey, after our host, the Dean of Westminster, had conducted intercessions in St. Faith's Chapel.

ARCHBISHOP WILLIAM TEMPLE

The Archbishop of Canterbury, Dr. William Temple, attended the first meeting and delivered an introductory address. In it he enunciated two principles which gave direction to our subsequent labours, and stand out clearly in our Report.

(1) The message of the Church is the Eternal Gospel. This remains fundamentally the same, from first to last. The Gospel could not alter, although the setting in which it was given, and the method of its presentation, could and did.

(2) The first need in evangelism is for a strengthening and a quickening of spiritual life within the Church: "We cannot separate the evangelisation of those without from the rekindling of devotion within."

As we cannot deliver into his hands the completion of the task which he entrusted to us, we desire to dedicate this Report to his memory.

There is an added reason for our so doing. The captions from his writings which introduce the chapters of the Report, indicate what we discovered, namely, that on every aspect of evangelism he had already said better what we wished to say.

It is due to his memory that this fact should be widely known.

As he sometimes complained, the newspaper reports of his sermons and addresses presented him to the public, almost exclusively, as a great Christian social reformer. The people of England are not sufficiently aware that his love for his fellow-man was constrained by a deep love of Christ, and emerged naturally from the heart and mind of a great evangelist who knew the message, had personal experience of its truth, and was himself a mission preacher.

Seeing that the members of the Commission numbered no less than fifty, and were drawn from all over England in days when travel was most difficult, the preliminary work was allotted to various committees which any member had the right to attend.

1. Members of the Commission in the North of England undertook to provide memoranda on:—

(1) *The Gospel and its Presentation.*

(2) *The Fellowship of the Church.*

2. Members of the Commission within reach of London prepared material on the following subjects:—

(1) *The Situation before the Church.*

(2) *The Human Agents of Evangelism.*

(3) *Methods of Evangelism.*

The London Committees continued to meet throughout the fly-bomb menace, though on one occasion a member was summoned by telephone to the ruins of his home.

3. There were also *ad hoc* Committees dealing with special aspects of evangelism:—

(1) *Modern Agencies for Evangelistic Propaganda.*

(2) *Evangelism by Advertising.*

(3) *Priests in Industry.*

(4) *The Return of Men and Women from War Service.* This last Committee prepared an *Interim Report,* which the Commission published and presented to the Church Assembly.

4. The Commission discovered that a Report on Evangelism could not provide the space necessary for the specific help and detailed suggestion that many in the Church were expecting with regard to practical methods of evangelism. It therefore asked the Church of England Youth Council to prepare a pamphlet on *Evangelism and Youth,* and authorised the formation of four Committees (with co-opted members) to produce pamphlets on *Parochial Missions, General Campaigns, Personal Dealings,* and *Evangelism among Children.* As the Commission will have reported before the pamphlets are in print, we hope that the Central Council for Evangelism, which we recommend, will become responsible for these Committees and their work.

The full Commission has met four times for sessions of not less than three days each, to discuss and formulate the material thus prepared. It has also held four one-day meetings.

A Drafting Committee of seven was appointed. It spent a week, and subsequently a further three days, in giving the Report that final shape which it owes chiefly to the perspicacity of the Bishop of Whitby.

ACKNOWLEDGMENTS

The Commission is deeply indebted to the Board of the Church Army, not only for providing accommodation for a three days session and for most of its many meetings in London, but for seconding Captain L. W. Chidzey (one of our members) in order that he might become the Secretary of the Commission. The Commission could not have accomplished its task without his organising ability and indefatigable energy.

Our thanks are also due to our Assistant Secretary, Miss Crusoe, who kept all the members fully supplied with memoranda and draft reports from the various committees; to the Rev. C. J. Offer, the Rector of Ightham, Kent, for preparing the Bibliography for acceptance by the Commission; and to Messrs. Parrett & Neves, Ltd., of Chatham, for working overtime to print the Report without the delays inseparable from war conditions.

THE PURPOSE OF THE REPORT

In presenting our Report we realise, of course, its limitations. It is written primarily for members of the Church Assembly, and for the clergy and laity whom they represent. But there is, literally, a whole world of difference between the outlook of such instructed Christians and that of the mass of our countrymen, whom we hope and pray our Report will ultimately affect.

Our purpose throughout has necessarily been to stimulate evangelism, not directly to evangelise. It is for the Church Assembly, and those whom they represent, to communicate in our disintegrated society the saving truths of the Gospel, in many different idioms and at many different levels.

The need is as urgent as the task is formidable. It will certainly require most patient learning, as well as most patient teaching. But it is only one aspect of the continual call to the Church to be re-created, by the Spirit of the Incarnate, at the very heart of human need, as age succeeds age.

In conclusion, we would testify to an unmistakable sense of being united and guided by the Holy Spirit.

From the first we realised that only a fellowship of prayer could enable fifty strangers to each other to discover the will of God for the Church, as it seeks to present Christ Jesus to men in days of unparalleled confusion. For that reason we decided at our first meeting that our sessions should be times of waiting upon God, as well as of conference; and we realise what we owe to the devotional addresses of the Rev. Jack Winslow, Father Algy Robertson, Canon P. C. A. Carnegy and Canon Roger Lloyd.

Our Report, too, is the proof of the contention we make therein, that the purpose of evangelism is itself the supreme unifying factor, blessed of the Holy Spirit, for creating fellowship.

Archbishop Temple never expected us to produce a unanimous Report. He expressed himself as prepared to receive two or three Reports, as long as they made revolutionary suggestions.

To our surprise, the question of more than one Report has never arisen.

We agreed that the Report with its recommendations should represent the considered opinion of the Commission *as a whole,* and not be taken to mean the subscription of each individual member to its every sentence or paragraph.

We agreed, also, that a signatory was entitled to dissociate himself, or herself, from any particular finding or recommendation; and that the fact should be noted if particularly desired. With these provisoes, I have the honour to present, on behalf of your Commission, our unanimous Report.

Christopher Rotten:

Whitsuntide, 1945.

(Chairman)

CONTENTS

CHAPTER I

THE SITUATION BEFORE THE CHURCH

"We must still claim that Christianity enables us to 'make sense' of the world, not meaning that we can show that it is sense, but with the more literal and radical meaning of making into sense what, till it is transformed, is largely nonsense—a disordered chaos waiting to be reduced to order as the Spirit of God gives it shape. Our problem is to envisage the task of the Church in a largely alien world."

WILLIAM TEMPLE.

Evangelism defined.

" To evangelise is so to present Christ Jesus in the power of the Holy Spirit, that men shall come to put their trust in God through Him, to accept Him as their Saviour, and serve Him as their King in the fellowship of His Church."

WE accept this definition, given by the *Archbishops' Committee of Inquiry on the Evangelistic Work of the Church*, which reported in 1918, emphasizing the truth that *to serve Christ as King* involves the duty of extending His Kingdom in the world. With this as our aim, our first task must be to examine the situation in which the Church is called to evangelise to-day.

The problem of modern evangelism.

2   In our terms of reference we were asked "to survey the whole problem of modern evangelism, with special reference to the spiritual needs and prevailing intellectual outlook of the non-worshipping member of the community." Such a diagnosis of the religious condition and outlook of the nation is very necessary before the Church can plan "definite action" to meet the spiritual needs of present-day men and women. To understand what is wrong is halfway to finding the remedy; to act without understanding is to invite failure. There are, however, obvious limits to what can be attempted within the space at our disposal. We cannot aim at providing an exhaustive and scientific analysis of an admittedly complex and confused situation. This matters the less since there are a number of good books available dealing ably with the subject.[1] It is not necessary to produce another such treatise. Rather, our purpose must be to fasten upon those points which seem to us to be of particular im-

[1] See Bibliography, p. 157.

portance for our inquiry, and to deduce from them certain conclusions as to how the Church can meet, courageously and hopefully, the situation thus revealed. In so doing, we realise that we must inevitably incur the charge of superficiality and overgeneralization.

England, still Christian on the surface.

3   What then are the conditions which constitute the "problem of modern evangelism."?

Seen from a distance, Britain is the country which seems most nearly to approach the ideal of a Christian community. The ceremony of the Coronation, the regular opening of sittings of Parliament with prayer, the Mayor's chaplain, the provision for religion in the Services and in all State institutions, the religious articles in popular periodicals, the Religious Department of the British Broadcasting Corporation, and many similar phenomena, go to show that the ethos of the State remains Christian. Delegates. for example, from the Protestant French churches at the Oxford Conference in 1937 on *Church, Community and State,* were at first shocked and then enviously astounded at the relations in this country between Church and State. They regarded the State as the Great Beast in Revelation. With us, the Established Church is "still entwined by countless subtile threads around the life of the realm and nation." The English are still more deeply influenced by Christianity than they themselves know, or churchgoers often admit. There is in them a fundamental soundness of character and a sense of responsibility that explains why other nations look to this country for leadership. But behind this façade the situation presents a more ominous appearance.

THE DRIFT FROM RELIGION

The gulf between Church and Nation.

4   There can be no doubt that there is a wide and deep gulf between the Church and the people. How far the rift has gone, or how deeply it has as yet affected national character, cannot be measured with statistical accuracy. Conditions vary surprisingly from area to area, and reports from personal observations differ widely according to the locality, or the section of the community, from which observers draw their conclusions. The war, however, with its general mix-up of the population, has afforded un unequalled opportunity of gaining some general appreciation of the situation. Thus, evacuation has opened the eyes of one half of the inhabitants of this island to see how the other half lives, with the result of eyes being opened very wide indeed. Then

again, men and women congregated together for war service present a cross-section of British society between the ages, roughly, of 18 and 40 years. Though they are living under abnormal conditions and are subject to special moral and emotional stresses, they remain essentially the product of our day and generation. The evidence, therefore, of chaplains and others in close touch with all three Services, and with munition factories, may be accepted as conclusive. They testify with one voice to the fact of a wholesale drift from organised religion. The present irrelevance of the Church in the life and thought of the community in general is apparent from two symptoms which admit of no dispute. They are (1) the widespread decline in church-going; and (2) the collapse of Christian moral standards.

1. The Decline in Church-going

5   It is indisputable that only a small percentage of the nation to-day joins regularly in public worship of any kind. Though accurate statistics are hard to obtain,[2] it is significant that matters usually appear to be at their worst where there is no conscious community life. The most depressing reports come from large industrial cities, and from that wide and heterogeneous belt of population which sprawls round London and includes about one-sixth of the total inhabitants of England. In provincial towns and comfortable suburbs (more particularly in the North) the decline in church-going is often less pronounced; though even here there is little cause for satisfaction. Conditions, however, vary surprisingly from parish to parish: the main determining factor being, apparently, the personality of the incumbent. More particularly is this the case in villages where a spiritual leader can often make an astonishing difference.   *Few Church-goers.*

6   The obvious fact of the decline in church-going throws into high relief the need for finding new means whereby a hearing may be gained for the Gospel message. It is plain that pulpit preaching can no longer be relied on as the principal medium for evangelisation. You cannot convert people who are not there. It is true that certain preachers have always been able to exercise an evangelistic ministry through the regular services of their churches, to which they have drawn large numbers of the unconverted. But definite   *Evangelising non-Church-goers.*

2 It has been recently estimated that from 10% to 15% of the population are closely linked to some Christian church; that 25% to 30% are sufficiently interested to attend a place of worship upon great occasions; that 45% to 50% are indifferent to religion though more or less friendlily disposed towards it; while 10% to 20% are hostile. (See *Christian News Letter*, 10th Feb., 1943, and Supplement 172 on *Religion and the People* by Mass Observation). It is open to question which is the more alarming feature, the failure of the Church to attract or its failure to repel.

evangelism has increasingly become associated with other means. Such means are parochial missions, individual contacts made in the course of the ordinary pastoral ministrations of the clergy, and the intercourse of converted Christian people with their fellows. They will all come under review in this Report, together with the possibilities afforded by other ways and means as yet untried or little known.

2. THE COLLAPSE OF CHRISTIAN MORAL STANDARDS

The increase of moral depravity. 7   Depravity is a sure symptom of spiritual disease. The war has revealed, and also accelerated, a sharp decline in truthfulness and personal honesty, and an alarming spread of sexual laxity, and of the gambling fever. Religious leaders of all denominations have drawn attention to the gravity of the situation in their public utterances and in the Press. Magistrates have expressed their anxiety at the rise (in the serious nature as well as in the quantity) of juvenile crime. School teachers complain of the difficulty of impressing upon their young charges the abomination of lying and stealing which they copy from their elders at home. The Government has found it necessary to resort to poster propaganda against venereal disease, and to issue to all medical officers of health a circular on the problem of illegitimate babies.

In the past 30 years the number of divorces has risen from upwards of 500 a year to approximately 12,250 in 1944.[3] In the summer of 1943, the Minister of Health sounded the alarm when he spoke of a "widespread moral collapse" in a large section of our young people. Though war conditions have certainly accelerated sexual promiscuity, the Registrar General's figures for marriages and births for 1938 showed that prior to the war fornication was as prevalent before marriage as adultery after it.

The "double standard of morality" for men and women, against which Josephine Butler contended so nobly, no longer obtains. Instead, owing to the immunity which contraceptives and prophylactives promise, the "man's standard" is increasingly being adopted by both sexes. The present depravity can cause no surprise when we recall the sex-obsession that has demented a disillusioned people since the last war. Few greater wrongs could have been inflicted on adolescents than the ubiquitous sex-suggestion of hoardings, plays, films, novels and ordinary conversation. It has

3 See the *Daily Telegraph*, Dec. 18th, 1944.

been continuous propaganda for sex-indulgence. Bawdy shows, for example, provided for men and women on war service, have been a shameful feature of the present war and an insult to their audiences who have often resented them.

8   If we have seemed to emphasize the declension from Christian moral standards more particularly in the realm of sex, it is because it is most obtrusive in this field, not because it is not marked in other directions. In every department both of public and private life the same trend is clearly to be seen. The gravest feature in the whole situation is that there is so little feeling of shame in loose living, still less in untruthfulness or dishonesty. The sense of responsibility and of duty has become undermined. There is no longer a generally accepted moral standard by which men judge their own actions. Instead, they excuse themselves by an appeal to a pseudo-scientific determinism. Personal failings are dismissed as the result of repressions, or as due to the action of the ductless glands. Dishonesty in private or public affairs is waved aside as the inevitable result of the economic system. The idea of man as a responsible person is in danger of disappearing with the loss of belief in a living God. No wonder our generation has been dubbed the Age without Standards. *An age without standards.*

9   There is, however, another side of the picture. Despite all adverse influences, the fundamental virtues are still manifested by the men, women and young people of our generation. Welfare workers tell of great numbers of young men and women (more particularly in the Forces) whose determined uprightness of life against the full force of suggestion is beyond all praise. The fortitude and self-sacrifice, the cheerful endurance and helpful comradeship, displayed in the Services and by the civilian population alike, which shone out from the dark days of 1940 (when England stood alone as the bulwark of freedom) astonished the whole world. *English character the heritage of the past,*

The past century, too, has been pre-eminently the most humane age in history. The contrast between the "Hungry Forties" of Charles Dickens' time and the England of to-day, shows an advance in the social, political and economic status of the masses with which no other epoch can compare. Ours is a closely knit society, with an inherited ideal of service for the community that runs like a golden thread through the fabric of English history. Our people are fundamentally decent and kindly. They would not wilfully inflict injury on another even if they have forgotten why.

but will it survive ? *10*   The vital question that has to be answered is, "Why has such a drift from the Christian religion occurred in a people of this nature? What has caused them to lose their hold upon the faith from which they have, in fact, derived the characteristics which they most generally prize?" To this question the right answer must be found, before the right action can be taken to ensure that its traditional virtues will continue to mark our race. For, as Sir Richard Livingstone warns us: "The philosophy of life, the standards by which the Victorian and earlier ages were governed, have broken down. We are left with traditions and habits of conduct inherited from them, as the earth may for a time still receive light from an extinct star. But that light will not continue to shine, nor can those habits and traditions long survive the beliefs from which they grew. Those who reject Christian beliefs cannot count on keeping Christian morals."[4]

UNDERLYING CAUSES

A diagnosis. *11*   We proceed, therefore, to a diagnosis of the causes that underlie the present situation. Throughout our enquiry we must be careful to distinguish between the universal and the particular; between what is common to all human nature and what is peculiar to our own generation. In discussing difficulties manifest in a certain age it is easy to fall into the error of regarding them all as the product of that age; whereas many of them may be due to the defects of fallen human nature in all ages. With this distinction in mind, how are we to set about disentangling the strands which have wrought the mental outlook of our generation, with its undoubted drift away from the Christian faith and life?

HUMANISM THE AGE-LONG LIE

The self-centred life. *12*   Humanism is the word now commonly used to describe that view of life which sees in man the source of all meaning and value, instead of in God. All down human history these two attitudes to life have been in conflict. The conflict is set forth in the first three chapters of Genesis, in which the human race is represented as having succumbed to the temptation of choosing the false and self-centred attitude to life: "your eyes shall be opened, and ye shall be as God."[5] This exaltation of self into the place which is

4 *Education for a World Adrift*, pp. 24, 25.
5 Gen. iii. 5.

God's is the root sin. The historic fact that man *has* made himself the centre of his universe constitutes the "Fall of Man."

13   In the mediæval period this false view of life, so flattering **The Middle** to man's self-esteem, was actively challenged, and to some extent **Ages.** kept in check, by the structure of society itself. The structure had been evolved at the close of the Dark Ages through the agency, and under the leadership, of the Church. Society, with its feudal system and its guilds, was organised on a basis at once functional and vocational. Privilege was there in plenty, but always linked to responsibility. Every man (no matter what his class level) had his recognised place in society, together with the status and self-respect which such recognition confers. However humble his function, he could recognise it as a necessary function: as necessary as any other, however exalted. His service was not simply *to* his master but *through* his master. Society as a whole represented a pyramid. Each level seemed to serve the one above it, and the apex of the whole was God Himself.

Unhappily the mediæval system was not in reality as Christian as men imagined it to be. While it expressed the true meaning of life as a co-operation to give expression to the will of God, *socially* it denied the brotherhood and freedom of man. By reason of the caste nature of feudalism, the individual (for the most part) was refused that ascent from one level to another for which his natural abilities might qualify him. More than this, the system concentrated power at the higher levels of the social pyramid, with all the opportunities for injustice and exploitation this affords. In the realm of *economics*, its system was based upon the right theory that, in the economic field, what has to be considered is what God would have us do, not what happens when God is forgotten. But its practice was too inelastic for the needs of an expanding commerce. In the *intellectual* sphere, the system attributed an undue finality to its own magnificent achievement, and thus brought about an arrest of history, by seeming to set a limit to the range of possibility open to the mind of man.

14   Because of the rigid system of subordination inherent in **The** mediæval Christendom, the Renaissance, when it came, was hailed **Renais-** as a revolt against the tyranny of the Church. The humanistic **sance.** view of life, "Man the measure of all things," was acclaimed as the creed of freedom and progress, while the Christian faith was suspect as cramping and reactionary. The assumption, so common to-day among non-Christians, that they alone are progressive or intellectual, and that education and science have "debunked" the Christian faith, is no new thing. It comes in uninterrupted descent from the days of the collapse of the mediæval system. As with this assumption in particular, so with Humanism in general, it is hard to understand why men still persist in being deluded by its specious and thread-bare creed. Seen in retrospect, the record of Humanism is not inspiring. Freed from the restraints of mediæval Christianity, it sweeps on, its crest rising ever higher and higher, and yet leaving in its wake the wreckage of promises invariably unfulfilled. "Man never is but always to be blessed," might be written large across its history.

The Age of Reason. 15   The renunciation of Humanism, which should have resulted from its dreary record of consistent failure, has been avoided (or at least postponed) by each successive age placing in men's hands some new tool or weapon which has renewed their hope. "After all," its devotees have argued, "the creed was sound enough; it was only the necessary power to give it effect which has been lacking, *and now we have it.*"

The French Revolution. 16   In the era of the French Revolution, the weapon of political power, now at last in the hands of the people, was confidently expected to bring heaven upon earth in an Age of Reason. It was, indeed, as good as done. The Abbé Sieyès declared that it would only take a fortnight, "since it is now merely an affair of politics, a science which I flatter myself I have mastered." The same naïve and exaggerated hopes of what political action could achieve is also reflected in English history, notably in the hopes fostered by the Reform Bill of 1832, and by each successive extension of the franchise.

The Industrial Revolution. 17   In the first half of the last century there was another great renewal of hope in the power of Humanism to bring salvation upon earth. It was occasioned by the invention of the steam engine. Thenceforth want was as good as abolished.

The one-time proletariat would soon sit every man under his vine—produced in Birmingham, and under his fig tree—produced in Lancashire. More glorious still, through the medium of international trade, war would be for ever unthinkable. Man, who at the outset of the Renaissance claimed his independence of nature, now proclaimed his dominance over it; and sang his *Me Deum* in the words of Swinburne's *Hymn of Man*: "Glory to man in the highest! For man is the master of things." Again, the "frantic boast" of Humanism proved a gigantic delusion. True, all the instruments in which man trusted—power production, communications, foreign trade—exceeded his wildest dreams. But as for an age of universal plenty, something must have gone wrong in the Hungry Forties, as also in 1929, when a financial blizzard began to sweep the world. While, in a world in which war was to be impossible, it is disconcerting to read what happened in the years 1854, 1857, 1859, 1864, 1866, 1870, 1898, 1903, 1914 and 1939; and there are other wars to chronicle besides these during the promised reign of peace.

18 We come to our own age—heir, as every age must be, to all that has gone before. Through it, too, there runs the same age-long struggle between the two philosophies of life. But what are the new factors changing the visage of our own generation? On the one hand, the creeds of the all-sufficiency of human nature, and of automatic evolution and progress of mankind, have received powerful reinforcement. On the other hand, Humanism has sustained its severest shock since the fall of the Roman Empire.

The Present Scientific Age.

The Modern Reinforcement of Humanism

19 The reinforcement of Humanism has been occasioned by the stupendous advance of science and invention during the present century, the Age of Progress. If in Mid-Victorian times it could be said that "science has made God unnecessary,"[6] how much more reason have we to be dazzled by the power that has come into our hands? To form, however, a true estimate of the effect of scientific advance upon our generation, there are three further factors, resulting from it, that demand serious attention.

The Age of Progress.

I. INCREASING URBANIZATION

First, there is the revolutionary change in the distribution of population, as between country and town. A century ago, in 1840, (almost, that is, within living memory), only a quarter of England's fifteen millions lived in towns of over twenty thousand inhabitants. In 1881, seventeen and a half, out of twenty-six millions, of the population were living in towns. By 1891 the proportion had increased to twenty-one millions of the population, out

1. Urbanization.

6 Secularist League Manifesto, Liège 1865.

of twenty-nine millions; and the drift to the towns has steadily continued ever since. Thus, increasingly, the masses of our people have migrated from the influence of nature to be absorbed in the materialism of urban surroundings.

Its effect on youth.
20   The effect of this, more particularly in the impressionable years of childhood and youth, has been profound. In 1843, George Borrow wrote that he had "always found in the dispositions of the children of the fields a more determined tendency to religion and piety than amongst the inhabitants of towns and cities"; for "they are less acquainted with the work of men's hands than with those of God." For this reason many to-day believe that religious revival will come from the countryside. But while in Borrow's day three English children out of every four were born in rural areas, the proportion to-day is more than reversed.

Youthful imagination now receives its stimulus from the shop window, the newspaper placard, the cinema and cinema poster. Much that passes to-day for art and literature has, on the whole, proved a corrupter of youth.[7] The most popular art, that of the cinema, with its immense influence, is almost totally devoid of any Christian background. The cinema "has shown an apparently pleasant world of unbridled desire, of love crudely sentimental or fleshly, of vast possessions, of ruthless acquisition, of reckless violence, of incredible kindliness; a maelstrom of excitement played upon by the glamour of false emotionalism."[8] The road to speedy and spectacular riches for film magnates has been to popularise and be-glamour a distorted picture of the most degenerate aspects of a materialistic age; and an erotic film industry has been allowed to be the chief single influence to which the young have been subjected during their formative years.[9]

2.   SECULAR EDUCATION

One-sided education.
21   The second factor is the one-sided character of the education of the past generation, and its increasingly secular outlook. The general community is, indeed, far more widely instructed than any previous generation. But the whole trend of modern education has been increasingly towards the sciences, to the exclusion of the

---

7 Cf. The Report of the Archbishops' Commission on *Training for the Ministry* par. 8.
8 Dr. A. E. Morgan: *The Needs of Youth*, p. 242.
9 The experienced headmaster of a secondary school in a Northern industrial town recently warned a gathering of parents that in his opinion the constant cinema-going of their children—tantamount to four or five times a week—constituted a greater menace to the young to-day than drink and gambling combined.

humanities or the liberal arts. Indeed, the preponderance of higher education is on the lines of applied science. This fact has an important bearing upon the evangelistic task of the Church. It is true that the general outlook of scientists to-day is more congruous to the Christian view of life than perhaps ever before: but a scientific education, of necessity, inculcates a mental habit which does not predispose to a Christian view of life. It is an axiom of scientific training that nothing must be taken on trust. It upholds (and rightly within its own sphere) a sceptical temper towards all hypotheses which have not been tested on a factual basis, and cannot be demonstrated as true with mathematical certainty. Further, and more far-reaching in its moulding of mental habit, science trains its votaries to look for the *How,* and to disregard the *Why;* to concentrate on *means* and to ignore *purpose.* *Homo* thus ceases to be *Sapiens* and, becomes *Sciens.*

22   Experience proves what we could only expect—namely, that **A barrier to faith.** an overweighted scientific education tends to produce a mentality which inevitably finds it hard to appreciate the importance which the Christian lays upon faith as a primary necessity, or his insistance that it is "purpose" and not "mechanism" which is of first importance. The cumulative result of modern education is, thus, to reinforce the humanistic view of life, if only by making it harder for man to understand and to accept the Christian faith.

23   Religious education, meanwhile, has steadily receded into **Religious Education.** the background, despite promising efforts to check an ebbing tide. It is true that the public schools "have preserved for English education a belief . . . in the essential part to be played by religion in education."[(10)] It is true, also, that Church Schools, though diminishing in number, have kept the same principle alive in national education. And it is true that in Council Schools there have always been found many good Christian teachers who have sincerely and devotedly tried to train children in the Christian way of life. But they have laboured under grave disadvantages and been hampered by many restrictions. It cannot be said that the national system has allowed Christian teaching to take its proper place as the unifying factor in education, co-ordinating all learning, inculcating a sense of responsibility, revealing the meaning and purpose of life. Indeed, the whole country was so shocked at the amount of the sheer pagan ignorance among the youthful

10 *The Fleming Report,* 1944, p. 44 (H.M.S.O.).

products of elementary and secondary schools which evacuation disclosed, that the long and persistent efforts of Christian education-alists have received recognition in the Education Act, 1944. We welcome the place in education that religious instruction and worship has thereby been given. More particularly we rejoice that, although these were more or less customary in most schools before the Act, they are now a matter of statutory obligation in all schools, and are thus accorded that recognised position of importance which should ensure their efficient and effective operation.

The encouragement of scepticism. 24   If we have to confess that education has become increasingly secular, scepticism has increasingly characterised educational technique. The individualism of the last century fostered the ideal of the completely undogmatic teacher, who thus (often unconsciously) inculcated an all-embracing scepticism in unreflecting youth. The notion was fostered that everyone was entitled to his own truth, and that (in the last resort) one belief was probably no truer than another. The consequence is only too apparent in the prevailing intellectual outlook. In the sphere of wisdom, the young cannot be expected to rediscover for themselves, unaided, those moral and spiritual truths which have been proved over and over again by the accumulated experience of past generations. The agnostic vacuum has inevitably been filled, and the refusal to teach children dogmatic religion has, in fact, amounted to teaching them the paramount importance of the economic appetites which so obviously dominate the world outside their schools.

It has, also, been forgotten that true Christian education is far more than to teach a certain subject at a certain time. It is a particular kind of education in all subjects and at all times—not only in the classroom. In other words, Christian education means schools with every activity pervaded by religion. But from at least the last quarter of the nineteenth century onwards, our national system of education has ruled that the young should contrast their childish memories of mother's knee religion with their knowledge of science or politics acquired at an adult level.

The cumulative effect has been that masses of our young people have lost a whole dimension of life—the spiritual dimension. They seem neither to be conscious of being spirit, nor to possess the faculty for apprehending the realms of the spirit.

3. MECHANIZED THINKING

25   The third factor in the reinforcement of Humanism is the appearance of the mechanistic mind. If scientific discovery and invention gave birth to the Industrial Revolution, the Industrial Revolution has, in turn, given birth to the Machine Age and has manufactured a mechanically minded nation. In an article, *The Perils of a purely Scientific Education*, the late Dr. William Temple foretold that such an education must produce a generation adept in dealing with things, indifferently qualified to deal with people, and incapable of dealing with ideas. To-day we are in a position to realise the truth of his warning. There is a large section of our people, whom it would be more accurate to describe as *mechanically*, rather than *scientifically*, educated. They may be highly trained and skilled mechanics. Within narrow limits their brains work keenly and quickly. They think clearly and originally about problems concerned with their craft; and many of them teach mechanics admirably. And yet great numbers, even of the most able among them, are incapable of reasoning or thinking clearly on abstract subjects, such as politics or religion. Professor T. E. Jessop, after an exceptionally wide experience with the Forces, and speaking as a psychologist, has diagnosed their mentality as definitely lacking in the necessary apperception for apprehending abstract ideas: "It is not that they won't; it is that they can't." Here, obviously, is a new factor in the present situation, and one of primary importance.

Evangelism, before it can gain an intelligent hearing, is confronted with the prior task of stimulating into activity, among a large section of the non-worshipping members of the community, mental powers which have been allowed to atrophy. Hence, the contention of the Bishop of Carlisle that "for a revival of religion there is needed a great rebirth of poetry and of the highest literature."[11]

THE MODERN EXPOSURE OF HUMANISM

26   We turn from the reinforcement which the humanist view of life has received in our times, to the shock which it has recently sustained. It is the shock of shattering disillusionment. The trust in human progress (evidenced in the last war by the high hopes we entertained of a better social order) has been pulverised by the

3. The mechanistic mind.

"Man . . . everywhere in chains."

11 See *York Journal of Convocation*, May, 1944, p. 47.

brutal logic of events. Instead of man being "the master of things," he finds himself their slave—the serf of the very civilization that he has created, and the powerless victim of mechanical laws of his own devising. It is not man who has been set free, but the blind materialistic forces he has unleashed. The machine has taken charge of its directors and reduced the common people to mere cogs in its wheels.

Industrial slavery.

27 In industry, irresponsible centres of economic power—international in their scope—exercise a virtual tyranny over the lives of masses of men. Between the two wars what economists (in their failure to make sense of the runaway process) termed cycles of fluctuation and financial blizzards, occasioned the macabre misery of starvation in the midst of plenty, and condemned honest workmen to an awful sense of insecurity. At that time unemployment produced a settled apathy (political and social as well as religious) among multitudes of the most alert and self-respecting sections of the community. It had to be witnessed to be believed. Then, too, the soullessness of the present industrial system, with its huge combines, has opened the door to evil forces which have infected its structure. For example, the only forms of employment open to many men and women are such as deprive them of that sense of vocation and public service which is their birthright.

Political autocracy.

28 In politics, the ordinary citizen feels he has no real say in the government of the country and is restive lest bureaucracy should break up his home life.

These are the days of Great Society in which social techniques have increasingly concentrated power in the hands of the few, and discouraged enterprise and creative individuality on the part of the many. The Englishman, with his innate independence of character, can never be happy to become a cipher among undifferentiated millions, living on the top of each other in a mechanised community. To this situation is due, more than is realised, the present-day collapse of morals. The need for self-expression has been so frustrated that it finds its easiest outlet in sex-indulgence.

War.

29 Finally, the outbreak of a second World War, after an uneasy truce of twenty-one years' duration, brought home to man how irrational is human nature, as well as the failure of the weapon of political power to "ring in the thousand years of peace." It confronted him, instead, with the hellish might of

scientific invention when turned, almost exclusively, to the work of destruction.

A FIELD OF OPPORTUNITY

30   It must not be supposed that disillusionment in the myth **Disillusion-**
of human progress affords a *positive* help to the work of evangel- **ment.**
ism.   Rather it tends, if not to a revolt, at all events to a settled
apathy which sweeps religion (with all other accepted beliefs) into
the rubbish bin.   When, for example, the Carnegie Trust investi-
gators, asked young unemployed miners in South Wales about
religion, the reply was: "What does it matter?"

31   None the less, the prevailing condition of disillusionment **An empty**
does at least present a field of opportunity.   Man, created for God, **field.**
whether he is conscious of it or no, cannot long exist without finding
some outlet for his instinct for worship.   If he is not won to the true
God, he will espouse some false creed, or cause, into which he can
throw himself.   The opportunity, therefore, afforded by the empty-
ing of disillusionment is bound to be fleeting. At the moment the
field is open.   Already there is discernible an increasing readiness
to discuss religion.   It is evidenced by the response to Padre's
Hours in the Forces, and to similar opportunities for informal discussion that have been provided in parishes.   Much the same report
comes from the universities where, it has been said, young men and
women who used to argue solely about Marx, now also argue about
God.   Rotary clubs and kindred associations afford a like experience.   Most revealing of all is the fact that during the past five
years the number of those who listen to the religious broadcasts of
the B.B.C. has increased by nearly fifty per cent, and the number
of those hostile or indifferent to them has decreased by thirty per
cent.   More and more people are prepared to give at least a hearing
to what the Church has to say.   **A field of**
                                                                     opportunity.

32   It would, indeed, be over-optimistic to regard the religious
condition of the country as already fallow ground, for much clearing
remains to be done.   At the same time, there are not wanting signs
that if the Church would speak with conviction and authority, the
nation would gladly hearken.   In that case, England would fulfil
its destiny to lead the world towards a new age.   As Dr. Mannheim
has asserted,[12] only "the rebirth of religion, both in terms of a

12 See *Diagnosis of our Times*. p. 106

popular movement and of regenerated leadership,'' will suffice for the reconstruction of man, and enable England to embrace the chance and the mission to develop a new pattern of society. Thus, "nothing matters more to the world and to the cause of the Divine Kingdom than that the Christian faith in England should again establish itself creatively at the heart of our people's daily life and interests."[13]

Can the Church rise to the opportunity?

33   In the face of the unique opportunity entrusted to our race, it would be fatal to minimise the problem that confronts the Church. We are called to a far harder task than to evangelise heathen who do worship (however ignorantly) a Power higher than themselves. In England the Church has to present the Christian Gospel to multitudes in every section of society who believe in nothing; who have lost a whole dimension (the spiritual dimension) of life; and for whom life has no ultimate meaning. The paramount spiritual need of the non-worshipping members of the community (as evidenced by this survey) is the recovery of their consciousness of God. Only so can they regain a doctrine of man morally responsible to God, and a philosophy of life that sees the material world as the sacrament of the realities of the Eternal. But the Church is ill-equipped for its unparalleled task and opportunity. The laity complain of a lack of creative leadership among all ranks of the clergy. The spiritual resources of the worshipping community are at a low ebb. Above all, the Church has become confused and uncertain in the proclamation of its message, and its life has ceased to reflect clearly the truth of the Gospel. It is for the Church, in this day of God, by a rededication of itself to its Lord, to receive from Him that baptism of Holy Ghost and of fire which will empower it to sound the call and give the awaited lead.

---

13 Dr. F. R. Barry: *The Relevance of Christianity*, p. 20.

CHAPTER II

THE GOSPEL

"The Gospel is true always and everywhere, or it is not a Gospel at all, or true at all."
                                                    WILLIAM TEMPLE.

W HAT has the Church wherewith to meet with confidence *The content* the situation thus revealed? There is only one answer: *of the* the Eternal Gospel, "the whole counsel of God." We *Gospel.* would emphasise these two epithets "eternal" and "whole" as applied to the Gospel. The Gospel for this twentieth century is identical with the Gospel which Jesus "came preaching," and the Apostles "went forth, and preached everywhere." Neither may we pick and choose particular aspects of this whole Gospel— emphasising the love of God to the exclusion of its inevitable reverse, which (in Biblical terms) is "wrath," not "neutrality"; or uplifting Christ as an Heroic Leader or Social Reformer, but not as our Crucified Saviour. We profoundly dissent from the assertion that there is "an element in the message which changes with varying conditions."[1] On the contrary, we believe that the tendency to preach "another Gospel,"[2] or a partial Gospel, has been the weakness (not to say the sin) of the Church in our generation, more especially between the two wars, and accounts very largely for its failure in evangelism.

35   It is the *presentation* of the Gospel, not its *content*, that *The presen-* changes with succeeding generations and their varying conditions. *tation of* We have *so* to present Christ Jesus that the people of our par- *the Gospel.* ticular age may come to accept Him as Saviour and King. This calls for a presentation expressed in terms and images consonant with present-day thinking and experience; and may be said to constitute the chief problem of evangelism.

We, therefore, devote this chapter to answering two questions:

[1] Report of the Archbishops' Inquiry on the *Evangelistic Work of the Church* (1918), p. 11.
[2] Gal. i, 6-9.

C

1. What is the Eternal Gospel? It is useless to evangelise unless we know the content of the Evangel.

2. How can the Gospel be presented to our generation? It is useless to evangelise unless the Good News is understood by those to whom it is proclaimed.

THE ETERNAL GOSPEL

The Nature of God.

THE Gospel is the Gospel of God, the good news about God, His nature and His action.

The specifically Christian Gospel is good news of God revealed in Christ. It did not break upon the world without preparation, but as the culmination of a long process of the self-revelation of God to man.[3] This revelation is the *final* revelation of God's nature. This does not mean that there is no more to be learned about God. It means that His nature cannot be more *perfectly* brought within the range of man's understanding, than by the action of God in translating the mystery of His Being into the language of a Human Life: "In the beginning was the Word, and the Word was with God, and the Word was God . . . and the Word became flesh and dwelt among us . . . full of grace and truth . . . No man hath seen God at any time, the only begotten Son which is in the bosom of the Father, he hath declared Him.[4]

God is Love.

37   The good news which the Christian faith offers to the world begins, therefore, with the good news of God's nature. At the heart of the universe there is no "fortuitous concourse of atoms" but a living Being, personal, or rather supra-personal; Whose wisdom is the creative, sustaining and directive principle of all things; Whose nature is love; Whose will is goodness, truth, justice and righteousness. Thus, there is a purpose running through the whole of life, and that purpose is a purpose of love.

The soul of man has not to "struggle alone with what of courage it can command against the whole weight of a universe which cares nothing for its hopes and fears,"[5] but finds itself set to live within the providence of the Living God, Whose nature is love and Whose purpose is directed to the well-being, in the highest possible degree, of each and all of His children.

The Gospel is the good news that God is, and that God is love.

3 Heb. i, 1.   4 John i, 1, 14, 18.   5 Bertrand Russell.

38   The Gospel is not only good news of God's nature, it is also **God's re-demptive** good news of God's action.   God has done, and is doing, something **action in** which man is unable to do for himself, yet upon which man's true **human history.** and complete well-being for time and for eternity (in Scriptural language, his *salvation*) utterly depends.   The necessity for this action lies in the fact of the world being "under sin."[6]

39   Sin is not only individual wrong doing, whether by com- **Sin.** mission or omission. It is the fact, however brought about, of being "off the right course." The world has departed from the course for which it was created (that is, God's purpose for it) and has absorbed a basic principle of error into the whole direction of its life. Consequently it is unable to recover its right direction and all its striving can only lead it further along the wrong path. It progresses, but not towards its true goal for which it was created.

The Gospel is the good news that God has intervened and done for man that which man could not do for himself.

40   By the Incarnation of Jesus Christ, the Word made flesh, **The work** God entered upon the human level into human life and history, **of Christ.** and has thereby shown its true nature and true course.   Jesus, by His life of absolute correspondence with the will and purpose of His Father, lived under the conditions of a world of sin, has drawn upon and into Himself the evil principle of sin, and by His atoning death has finally overthrown it. By His Resurrection He has revealed the new levels of life opened to men by the power of His Atonement. By His Ascension He has closed the gap which had separated man from God. And by the consequent descent of the Holy Spirit He has given to men a power by which they may lay hold upon all the benefits of His redeeming work.

The Gospel is the good news that God was in Christ, reconciling the world unto Himself.[7]

41   This reconciliation results in the restoration of man to his **The King-** right place in the order of God's creation, an order broken by sin. **dom of God.** This order is one in which all creatures are rightly related to God the Creator, and therefore to one another. It is described in the Gospels as the Kingdom of God, or the Kingdom of Heaven. In Christ the Kingdom of God has "come upon"[8] men, and has been opened to all believers. The result of man's entry into the Kingdom

6 Rom. iii, 9.
7 II Cor., v, 19.
8 Luke xi, 20.

is that he is introduced to a complete series of new relationships, covering every department of life and activity.

The Gospel is the good news of the "restoration of all things"[9] in Christ.

Man's Response. Faith, *42* To enter into the Kingdom involves man's response. This response is described by two words, Faith and Repentance. The New Testament word Faith carries with it the idea of trust and also of the obedience which flows from trust; for the exercise of faith must always involve something in the nature of a leap in the dark. It is that trust in a person which shows itself in a readiness to obey his will.

and Repentance. *43* This in turn involves Repentance. Repentance is that change of outlook which comes about as trusting man finds his old outlook changing into that of the Teacher Whom he has come to trust. This change of outlook covers a wider field than is generally associated with the word repentance. Repentance is generally taken to mean a change of attitude to those things only which we know to be wrong. But true repentance, which springs from faith in Christ, will gradually be found also to involve a change of mind about much which we have heretofore assumed to be right.

God's acceptance of man's faith and repentance. *44* While both these activities, faith and repentance, will grow by being exercised, they will never, even at their highest, enable man to restore himself to that right relationship with God, and with God's creatures, which is the very nature of the Kingdom. Such restoration is the act of God alone. But by the sincere exercise of them, even in their earliest stages, man is admitted to all the benefits of Christ's redeeming work, and so finds the Kingdom lying open to him through Christ the Way.

The Gospel is the good news that God in Christ has opened the Kingdom of Heaven to all believers.

The fellowship of the Church *45* Christ came to set before every man the choice of accepting or rejecting this offer of participation in the Kingdom, which is *Salvation*. Acceptance must always be by the free act of the individual will. Though this act of will may be expressed in different ways, according to the circumstances of the individual making it, in all cases it must involve the readiness to confess Christ before men.[10] And since all this brings him into that widespread system of right relationships which constitutes God's Kingdom, it can never

9 Acts iii. 21.   10 Matt. x. 32.

be realised as a solitary life but only in community: a fellowship which transcends all barriers of language, race and class.

46   This fellowship is a supernatural thing. It is the creation of **The fellowship of the Holy Ghost.** God the Holy Spirit. His office is to bring to men the things of Christ.[11] By His descent upon men He brings to them the new life of the Risen Christ, the life which was ever in perfectly right relationship to His Father, and therefore to all God's children. Man's faith and repentance constitute the necessary attitude for the reception of the Holy Spirit. Those who thus receive Him become thereby the Church which is Christ's Body,[12] for they are living with His life. The Church is, therefore, the area in which this supernatural fellowship is operative.

47   The Church is thus integral to the Gospel, and true evangelism must always be a calling into its fellowship: "That which we **The Church, the Body of Christ.** have seen and heard declare we unto you also, that ye may have fellowship with us: yea, and truly our fellowship is with the Father and with his Son Jesus Christ."[13] By reason of its very nature, the Church cannot rest satisfied while any remain outside its fellowship. It is the Body of Him Who "willeth that *all* men should be saved, and come to the knowledge of the truth"[14] and therefore finds expression in missionary service to the world.

The Gospel is good news of the new life to be enjoyed in the fellowship of Christ's Church.

48   With new life comes new power. Life is the source of **Personal Power through the Holy Spirit.** power. No one can read the New Testament without recognising that such was the experience of the members of the fellowship. Not necessarily is it a power which enables its possessors to avoid suffering, or to bend events to their will. It is the power to transcend circumstances which resides in the Head of the Church, and thus to change their values and to turn them towards God's eternal purpose. It is the power to conquer sin in our own lives that sin should not reign in our mortal bodies.[15] And it is this consciousness of realised power which enables the believer to go on his way through this troublous world in the peace of God, "rejoicing in the power of the Holy Spirit."

The Gospel is good news of the power of the Holy Spirit available to the members of Christ.

11 Cf. John xvi, 14.
12 Eph. i, 23.
13 I John, i, 3.

14 I Tim., ii, 4.
15 Rom. vi., 12.

Eternal Life.

49   Since the life which is shared in the fellowship of Christ's Church is the life of Him Who was dead and is alive for evermore,[16] it cannot be destroyed by death. The whole proclamation of the Gospel in the New Testament is shot through and through with that truth. Those who are in Christ Jesus have already Eternal Life and can never die.[17] St. Paul sees the pledge of the resurrection of believers both in the resurrection of their Lord,[18] and also in their experience of the life of the risen Christ in their own lives.[19] They are even now sharing in the risen life. St. John sees the evidence of the present possession, by believers, of eternal life in the new quality of life displayed in their relations one to another: "We know that we have passed out of death into life, because we love the brethren."[20]

The Risen Life.

50   The Gospel thus gives to death itself a new significance. The good news of eternal life is no mere assertion of survival. It is the Gospel of the resurrection. The eternal life upon which the believer enters is the life of Him Whom "God raised up, having loosed the pangs of death: because it was not possible that he should be holden of it."[21] The peculiar character of that life is, therefore, that it is the *risen* life.[22] To enter upon it, the believer must first share in Christ's death. The foundation of the Christian life is a death to sin and a new birth to righteousness. We are baptised into Christ's death, that we may hereafter walk in newness of life.[19] This dying has to be re-enacted constantly as the condition of entry upon eternal life. Thus St. Paul speaks of "dying daily"[23] and of "always bearing about in the body the dying of Jesus, that the life also of Jesus may be manifested in our body."[24] Physical death becomes one great moment within this process, and is thereby transformed. Unlit and unredeemed by Christ, death is the last expression of the disappointments and frustrations which confront man at every stage of his life, and on a deeper level can be seen as sin's triumph. In Christ, death becomes the gateway to life, and so is given a positive value.

The Future Life.

51   Moreover, this Gospel of resurrection answers (in as explicit terms as are possible for man's temporal understanding) those questions which are natural to man's heart concerning the risen life of eternity. Much must remain beyond the scope of our

16 Rev. i, 18.
17 John vi, 47; xi, 26.
18 I Cor., xv, 12.
19 Rom. vi, 1-11; Phil. iii, 10, 11.
20 I John, iii, 14.

21 Acts ii, 24.
22 Col. iii, 1-3.
23 I Cor., xv, 31.
24 II Cor., iv, 10.

imagination. But both the teaching of Jesus, and still more His appearances after His resurrection, reveal the future life as a true personal life: a life in which, though changed, we remain ourselves, recognisable as such by those whom we have known and loved upon earth; a life with greater powers and opportunities of service than any we have possessed here; a life freed from the limitations which restrict and hamper us while yet in this mortal frame.

It is this truth which is enunciated, and preserved, in the Christian doctrine of the *Resurrection of the body*. The doctrine does not assert the physical reconstruction of this "body of our humiliation,"[25] but the risen life of the whole man—the perfected spirit "clothed upon" [26] in such measure as shall be perfectly proportioned to its new and heavenly glory.

The Gospel is the good news of redemption to Eternal Life.

52   Involved in this truth and essential to it, is the fact of **Judgment.** judgment to come. Judgment is the ultimate separation of the evil from the good, with the consequent destruction of all that opposes itself to God's will. Such must be the precursor and condition of unfettered life with God. The truth is enshrined in the Christian doctrine of the Second Coming of Christ in judgment. Judgment is committed to Him[27] because He is the Truth, the norm by which all judgment must be made. Of this He speaks in terms which are symbolical (as all terms must be which deal with ultimate truth) but of tremendous gravity: a gravity which runs through all the pages of Holy Scripture and, indeed, through all Christian thought. Judgment is no superstition or fiction. It is a tremendous and solemn truth. Ultimately all that is found valueless in God's sight must and will be abolished, that that which He can use may be set free, and "God may be all in all."[28]

53   Revelation and reason alike point to this inevitable consum- **"The end of all** mation. The idea of the inherent indestructibility of the human **things."** soul (or consciousness) owes its origin to Greek, not to Bible, sources.[29] The central theme of the New Testament is eternal life, not for anybody and everybody, but for believers in Christ as risen from the dead. The choice is set before man here and now. Though the announcement of impending judgment may not at first sight appear to be "good news," yet it is integral to the Gospel. It is the assertion of the final triumph of good and of the abolition

---

25 Phil. iii, 21.
26 II Cor., v, 2.
27 John v, 22.

28 I Cor., xv, 28.
29 Gore: *Belief in God*, p. 130, footnote.

of evil. Further, the Gospel is the good news that no man need fall under judgment, if he will accept the redemption freely offered to him in Jesus Christ: "There is therefore now no condemnation to them that are in Christ Jesus."[30]

The Gospel is the good news of the final triumph of the good, and that Jesus Christ has opened the way of escape from the power of sin, from the fear of judgment and from everlasting death.

The Presentation of the Gospel

Religion without Revelation? HOW is the Eternal Gospel to be presented to minds moulded by the conditions we have described in the previous chapter? Prof. Julian Huxley, in his book *Religion without Revelation,* wrote: "The modern man has a God-shaped blank in his consciousness." He spoke for a whole generation. The primary and fundamental difficulty in the way (wherever this generation is unable to accept the Christian revelation) is that it cannot grasp what is meant by revelation. The whole trend of post-renaissance thought has been more immanentist than transcendant. Men have tended to give to the word "God" (if they gave it any meaning at all) the connotation of something which emerges from, and is contained within, the universe of which man is a part. So it is that the great Biblical conceptions of a Living God, transcending His created world, "speaking" to it and "visiting" it, have been dismissed as anthropomorphic crudities.

The presentation to our generation. 55 Christian "revelation" carries with it all the great categories of God, sin, judgment, redemption and atonement, which are meaningless if the fundamental distinction between Creator and creature is once lost. Can the great concepts of the Gospel, which these terms embody, be expressed under new analogies and similes consonant with the thought forms of the modern mind? We feel bound to make some attempt to translate certain of the foregoing theological statements of the Eternal Gospel into language such as present-day hearers might themselves employ to express spiritual needs of which they are acutely conscious. In so doing, we cannot hope to do more than point the way to a far wider and more expert handling of a difficult and urgent task.[31]

[30] Rom. viii. 1, 2.
[31] "There is great need that full attention should be given to training ordinands in the power of translating the technical language of theology into terms understood by ordinary people." *The Report of the Archbishops' Commission on Training for the Ministry* (1944), par. 107.

THE NATURE OF GOD

56   The connotation often given to the word "God" is vague **GOD.**
in the extreme, and falls infinitely short of the Christian revelation.
The difficulty felt is generally due either to faulty teaching or to
misunderstanding. The idea (by no means rare) that the Church
presents God as "an old man with an old man's foibles, jealous,
irascible, unaccountable and very open to flattery," cannot be dismissed as insincere. Sometimes the impression has been given by
the unguarded or misunderstood expressions of a Christian teacher.
More often it is the effect of the reading, or the hearing, of the
language of the Bible and the Prayer Book by those unlearned in
its symbolism; or of an education which has been one-sided and
lacking in the humanities.

57   The real difficulty, however, lies deeper. It is rooted in a **A Living**
new and scientific type of Gnosticism[32] which, by concentrating on **Being.**
the manifold agencies of causation that mediate between the
creature and the Creator, virtually banishes God (as a living, loving
and sustaining Being) from His creation, and casts doubt upon
the efficacy of prayer.

The scientific mentality of the present day naturally demands
a rational demonstration of the fact of the living God. Accordingly,
the traditional and classic arguments for the existence of God have
special cogency for our times, if they are re-stated in terms of
modern knowledge, and if emphasis is laid upon the weight of
their cumulative testimony. But it must always be remembered
that the classic arguments do not pretend to do more than offer
a rational *basis* for faith. The obvious truth must also be driven
home that if there is a God, He alone can reveal to men the nature
of His Being.

THE MEANING OF SIN

58   Though there is to-day little consciousness of sin, men are **"The**
acutely aware of a sense of frustration and of discord, both in them- **present**
selves and in their relations with their fellow men. They are also **tent."**
very sensible of repeated failure and disappointment in their efforts
to escape from their discontents. In consequence, they experience

---

[32] The Gnostics were the earliest heretics. They were the "enlightened,"
whose superior knowledge interposed successive generations of emanations,
or spiritual beings, between God and the world. In proportion as these
emanations were nearer the world, and so more remote from their primal
source, the divine in them became fainter.

a condition which could not better be described than that of "having no hope, and without God in the world."[33]

It is a grim commentary upon our times that it requires a major war to restore some (temporary) sense of purpose to life. Moreover, it seems to many that the only explanation of their powerlessness to control each one his own life and its settings, must be the activity of unknown and malign agents (the mysterious "they") who are deliberately, for some ends of their own, bringing about the evil conditions of which they complain. Finally, as the climax of the general perplexity, there is the seeming inscrutability of the disaster which has come upon the world. This is illustrated by the avidity with which men will seize upon any theory which professes to offer a reasonable diagnosis of the world's malady, as, for instance, Marxism. Life simply does not make sense.

To men in this frame of mind the Gospel should make an immediate appeal, if it can be presented not only as revealing the root cause of their troubles, but also as assuring them that God has done, and is doing, that which man is so conscious of being unable to do. Such Good News would come as the best of good news if only it could be apprehended as true.

The sense of guilt.   59   Sin is apprehended by different people in very different degrees and under very different terms.

The *degree* of apprehension depends upon their spiritual insight. It is a commonplace that the profoundest apprehension of sin is to be found in the greatest of the saints.

The *terms* under which sin is apprehended depend upon the lines along which their mental processes have been developed. The simplest and most adequate description is that given in the General Confession. To a man who so apprehends his sinful condition, the very crown of the joy of restoration will lie in the removal of that sense of guilt which he recognises to be the consequence of his estrangement from God. But there are many who, in fact, share this experience of sin but do not recognise it in the terms set forth by Scripture. Though psychiatrists report that the sense of guilt is extraordinarily widespread, and accounts for the phobias of great numbers of their patients; few of these relate their distress to the fact that they are alienated from God. Yet their experience is the very one described in Bible language as "bondage under sin."

33 Eph. ii, 12.

60   Sin is far wider in scope than conscious wrong-doing. The **"Off the right course."** Greek word for sin comes from a root which means "missing the mark" or "being off the right course." Man deviates from the right course not only by conscious wrong-doing (by deed and by omission), but also through ignorance and by reason of the make-up of his fallen nature. Thus, while all conscious wrong-doing is sin, not all sin consists in conscious wrong-doing.

The degree of personal guilt involved in these different forms of sin varies immeasurably; but its effect remains the same, however brought about. A ship runs ashore. It makes all the difference to the pilot whether the cause was his own culpable negligence or the failure of the steering gear. But in either case the ship is equally ashore.[34]

Mankind, from whatever cause, has deviated from the right course, and is thereby in a state of divergence from the truth— the true order of the universe, which is God's. Therefore his very progress does not bring him nearer to his true goal. He is, quite literally, lost.

61   One chief obstacle to the acceptance of this doctrine of **God's pattern for all creation.** lost mankind by the mind of to-day lies in the doubt as to whether there is such a thing as absolute truth, or whether all truth is but relative.

A bridge over this gap may be found by reference to the fact that it is in its acceptance of an order or pattern in nature that science has found the secret of true progress. In a pre-scientific age men were always trying to write their own pattern across the face of nature. They made but little progress, and that little was due to their accidentally blundering upon the true order of nature. The immense advance of science dates from the acceptance of scientists of the fact of the order of nature, with the consequent corollary that their primary task was to study its pattern and to follow where it led.

Here is, at least, a significant analogy to the Christian's belief in a true pattern for all creation, which man must discover and follow if he is to attain to fullness of life. That true pattern is the will and purpose of God, its Creator. The clue by which we may follow it is the revelation given us in Christ, "even as the truth is in Jesus."

---

34 Cf. the distinction drawn by theologians between *formal* and *material* sin. See Dr. K. E. Kirk, " *Some Principles of Moral Theology*," p. 223.

The Fall.   *62*　　　God created all things in a harmony which should witness
to the glory of the Creator. Man, endowed with something of the
Creator's own attributes and created in His image, was destined
to act in the world as His vicegerent for the maintenance of that
order and harmony. But man prostituted his powers by using
them not for God's glory but for his own self-exaltation. Thereby
he arrogated to himself the position due to God alone.[35] This is
the very essence of sin, and the meaning of the Fall. But God
is not to be swayed from His purpose of love by man's sin. Since,
therefore, it is God (not man) Who rules the world, the clash between God's purpose and man's divergent will can only result in
human chaos.

THE FACT OF JUDGMENT

**Judgment
here.**   *63*　　　The chaos that thus results from self-will is, in effect, the
judgment of God. There is nothing arbitrary about God's judgment. It is the inevitable consequence of man's attempt to act
independently of God. And the judgment can be terminated only
when man is either removed from his place or reconciled to God.

　　　The idea of the judgment of God is one which our generation
finds it difficult to take seriously. Yet it is perfectly in accord
with contemporary experience. Our Lord sought repeatedly to
bring home to His hearers the fact of judgment by the use of
analogy. As He was speaking to an agricultural community He
used such pictures as that of the Wheat and the Tares. To our
mechanical age a more arresting analogy would be that of com-
ponents of a machine which do not come up to specification. Such
will work havoc in the machine. If it is to do its work, they must
be removed and scrapped. The Good News is that in Christ God
has provided an alternative. They can be re-made. Man need not
remain lost; he can be reconciled to God.

**Judgment
hereafter.**   *64*　　　Though the experience of life brings home to most thought-
ful people the fact of judgment here, the truth of judgment to
come, after death, is obscured by the indifference of so many to
the idea of any future life. It is not that they disbelieve in it but,
rather, that they are not even interested. In some this indifference is due to such an absorption in the vivid present that neither
the past nor the future has any factual reality or value for them.
With others it is occasioned by the profound belief (so conspicuous

35 Gen. iii, 5.

in the Old Testament) that the individual lives on into an indefinite future, in the happiness of mankind to which he contributes now. With others, again, the lack of desire for a future life grows naturally out of a confusion between the Christian doctrine of the resurrection to eternal life, and a doctrine of mere indefinite continuance of life as it is known in this world.

On the other hand, the general attitude of indifference to a future life is challenged by persistent inward questioning; as is shown by the interest, ever since the last war, in Spiritualism. The whole situation demands much clear and more insistent teaching on the Christian doctrines of the Communion of Saints, of Judgment and Eternal Life.

The Work of Redemption

65   Reconciliation with God can never be accomplished by man himself. Man's distinctive quality (that which makes him man) lies in his peculiar relationship to God, unique in all creation. Man is not simply as one of the creatures. His true centre is in God on the eternal level; even while he is, at the same time, a creature involved in the flux of time and of historical existence. The essence of man's sin lies in his attempt to find in himself, on the natural level, that centre for his being which, in truth, lies in God, in the eternal. **Original Sin.**

As self-centredness is the essence of man's sin, it follows that every effort that he may make (even towards the good, and particularly every successful effort), only confirms him in his root sin more completely, because it is made from this centre. Thus every new good which he achieves brings with it its own peculiar new evil. For example, even the attainment of humility, when regarded as his own achievement, produces in him the new sin of spiritual pride—pride in being humble. Such is the tragic quality of man's fallen nature, which we term Original Sin.

66   Once the truth of original sin is recognised, it reveals the essential falsity of the humanist's basic article of faith. Man can never, by a process of evolution or steady progression, find his way at last into the Kingdom of God, nor even into an earthly Utopia within history. The progress of history itself shares with man the tragic experience of exchanging old sins for new. **The new birth.**

Thus, if man is to reach the Kingdom of Heaven, there must be a discontinuity in his self-centred progress. It is this discontinuity of which the Bible speaks under the terms of death and resurrection: "a death unto sin, a new birth unto righteousness"; and its outcome is a "new creature." But newness of life can only come by God's intervention, not by man's own effort. What we term Salvation is God's free gift to man through Christ.[36]

Salvation. 67   Salvation is reconciliation with God. Considered with reference to the life of the individual, the result is the restoration of his own interior harmony. In the fashionable term of the moment it is an integrated or re-integrated personality.

In human life there are always present interior strains which, when they rise above a certain degree of intensity, manifest themselves as neuroses of which medical science can take cognisance. These strains find their origin in the fact that as man is created for God, the end to which his powers are truly adapted by their nature is the service of God. But man, being "under sin," is ever seeking to use these powers for other ends centring round himself. So doing, he creates a conflict within himself. When this conflict is resolved, the result is an access of power, since nothing is now being wasted.

As the root of the conflict lies in his attachment to himself, it is not in man's power to remove it. The removal must be done from God's side.

This explains Professor C. G. Jung's statement: "Among all my patients in the second half of life—that is to say, over thirty-five—there has not been one whose problem in the last resort was not one of finding a religious outlook on life. It is safe to say that every one of them fell ill because he had lost that which the living religions of every age have given to their followers, and none of them has been really healed who did not regain his religious outlook."[37]   It also explains why "religion is good for every craft." The complete integration of man's personality removes all waste, and releases all his powers for his work.

Atonement and Sacrifice

Was the Cross necessary? 68   The Christian knows that his reconciliation with God has been accomplished by the atoning life and death of Jesus Christ. But to the non-Christian this appears to have no relevance to his own situation. Even if God did so intervene in Christ, why should

---

36 II Cor. v, 14-21.
37 *Modern man in search of a soul*, p. 264.

His intervention take this form? How does it help him that an Innocent Man should die under such circumstances of injustice? How can the death of Jesus benefit him save as an example of faithfulness and fortitude?

69   Here, too, there is, readily available, a modern bridge over to the mental frame of the twentieth century. The product of our mechanically-minded age should find it particularly easy to recognise that when once something has gone wrong, more power is needed to make good the defect than would have been adequate had all gone well. If a motor car has been ditched, more power is required to extricate it than would be necessary to propel it along the road. Indeed, the extra power needed is more than its own engine can supply and must be provided from without. Sacrifice, the extra price,

It is not hard to see that this principle is of universal application, from the most trivial examples to the very greatest. War breaks out and the principle is seen at work on a vast and heroic scale. An incalculable extra price is demanded from the nation before peace can be restored. But this is nothing else than the law of sacrifice. Sacrifice is the *extra price* demanded before anything which has once gone wrong can be brought back to its normal. There is no escape from the operation of the law of sacrifice. "According to the law, I may almost say, all things are cleansed with blood, and apart from shedding of blood there is no remission."[38]

70   Man was created for the service of God. His powers were given him to that end, and are proportioned to that task. But once man has fallen from the right course, *extra power* (which he is powerless to supply) is needed to restore him. The extra power must come from God Himself, for there is no other source. And God Himself can only come to the rescue of His lost world by the path of sacrifice, for there is no other way. giving the extra power.

71   Christ Jesus, our Saviour, came into the world and lived the perfectly God-centred life. As a boy He proclaimed the purpose of His life: "Wist ye not that I must be about my Father's business?"[39] As a man, facing the Cross, He could declare to His Father: "I glorified Thee on the earth, having accomplished the work which Thou hast given me to do." The "offence" of the Cross.

---

38 Heb. ix, 22.   39 Luke ii, 49 (A.V.).

Here we are confronted with the offence of the Cross, as old as Christendom itself. Young people, particularly, of our humane age, are scandalized at the Scriptural emphasis on the inevitability of the Crucifixion, and at the Church's insistence in "dragging it in" and giving it such prominence. This repugnance to the idea of the sacrifice of the Cross, as something horrible and revolting, represents a regression to the old pagan worship of the beautiful—the pagan unwillingness to face the ugly.

But there *are* ugly things in life, and they do not cease to be so because we refuse to face them. They can only be removed by coming down to them and dealing with them, in the spirit of the physician or the soldier. That spirit we all admire. The Cross is the ultimate expression of that heroic spirit. It is God entering the lists of sacrifice. If He refused this, He could not embody the highest good. The martyr, the doctor, the soldier, would be higher than He. The Cross can be understood only in terms of sacrifice.

The Elder Brother. 72   Had the world been God-centred, as it was meant to be, the earthly life of the Incarnate Son of God would have presented a very pageant of requited love—the loved Elder Brother passing through the ranks of adoring younger brethren. But to live a God-centred life in a world which had departed from God, demanded of Christ the *extra price* of facing unflinchingly the pain of misunderstanding, hatred, jealousy, betrayal and death.

Redeeming Love. 73   It is a strange and tragic misunderstanding which has found in that life story a basis for the idea that love will always prevail upon earth, and that you can make men love you by loving them. On the contrary, the life of Christ shows unmistakably that the most perfect love can be unrequited, betrayed and rejected upon earth. But it is just that sacrificial love, in that it does not withdraw itself in the face of such betrayal, which becomes God's instrument for His supernatural purpose of redemption.

For the Cross is not the end. Christ rose victorious over death: "It is Christ Jesus that died, yea rather, that was raised from the dead, who is at the right hand of God."[40] The life offered on the Cross is committed into the Father's hands, and poured out by the operation of the Holy Ghost upon those who will receive it. Thus, there comes into being the fellowship of the Church.

[40] Rom. viii, 34.

The Fellowship of the Church

74   The good news of the Fellowship of the Church, created by **The con-**
the indwelling of God the Holy Spirit, should present no great **ception of**
difficulty to the men of to-day. They are familiar enough with the **community.**
conception of persons "dwelling in" one another, and deriving
fullness of personality from their organic relationship one with
another.

The old nineteenth century individualism has passed, and
has been succeeded by an emphasis on the social nature of personality. This emphasis is found throughout all ranges of contemporary
thought; from Professor A. N. Whitehead's suggestion that the
ultimate concept of reality may be found in organism,[41] to the
assertion of the most unthinking members of society that they
belong to their particular class "to the bone." On all hands we are
confronted with impressive manifestations of the power the conception of Community possesses to grip and dominate men's minds—
not the least being the phenomenon of Nazi-ism.

75   There is, however, a practical difficulty felt about the **The human**
Church by the non-worshipper, and it is a serious one. With the **element in**
doctrine of the Church as the fellowship of the Holy Spirit, we come **the Church.**
within the operation of the pragmatic test: "Does it so work out
in practice?" We cannot escape our Lord's own criterion: "By
their fruits ye shall know them."

**Ultimately the evidence for the credibility of the Gospel in
the eyes of the world must be a quality of life manifested in the
Church which the world cannot find elsewhere.**

Christ intended His Church, and its individual members, to
be His living epistles "known and read of all men," and interpreting to them the dogmas of the Faith in the contemporary idiom
of ordinary life.

Herein lies the tragedy of the failure of Church people
generally to display to non-worshippers a supernatural quality of
moral power and of brotherly kindliness.

Herein, too, lies the tragedy of the divisions of Christendom
itself. Quite undoubtedly the spectacle of rival churches presents
one of the greatest obstacles in the way of the acceptance of the
Church's witness: "We are faced with a variety of religious de-

41 *Science and the Modern World*, p. 80.

nominations . . . which . . . only succeed in neutralising each other's influence on the minds of the people."[42]

If for this reason only, evangelism at home must never be separated from missions overseas. In the missionary awakening of the nineteenth century we have an expansion of the Universal Church unparalleled in any previous age, and a phenomenon that can even claim to be the greatest event in modern history.[43] There, in the mission field, we see for our encouragement the triumphs of the World-wide Church, and what it can accomplish when the sheer weight of the forces of paganism compels the various missionary churches to co-ordinate their efforts in order to evangelise the world.

The Communion of Saints. 76   It must, of course, be conceded that the Divine cannot be manifested in all its fullness in the Church on earth. The Church is composed of men who are not yet "made perfect," but are themselves under the judgment of God in the tragic web of history, and stand very much in need of His mercy and grace. Even at its best, the Church must always appear a very mixed society, not a picture gallery in which every portrait is a masterpiece. The justification for the Church's existence lies not so much in the perfection of its members, as in its ability to point beyond itself to God. And the power of its witness will always be in direct proportion to the extent it is able to present to the world the spectacle of a fellowship on earth whose "citizenship is in heaven."

The Divine Society is not limited to this world. It forms a living fellowship with the saints of all ages. The fellowship of the Church is rooted in the unseen world. No saint ever passes out of that Body in which Christ is the life and love of all its members; and "the Church on earth grows with the vigour of those who have passed on into Paradise . . . for everyone who has been faithful unto death becomes an organic channel of the life of Christ, in Whom he lives, to the Body of Christ remaining upon earth."[44]

The Commission to Evangelise. 77   How is the Gospel, bearing these tremendous issues, to be proclaimed and brought home to the men and women of our generation? What hitherto unused resources are lying available to the Church's hand for the work of evangelism? How can the

42 Mannheim: *Diagnosis of our Times*, p. 21.
43 See John Foster, *Then and Now* (S.C.M.), chap. iv.
44 Father R. M. Benson, of Cowley.

Church by the quality of its fellowship, the assurance of its faith and reality of its worship, become a more effective instrument in the hand of its Lord? To a consideration of these questions we now address ourselves.

CHAPTER III

THE APOSTOLATE OF THE WHOLE CHURCH

"The evangelization of England. . . is a work that cannot be done by the clergy alone; it can only be done to a very small extent by the clergy at all. There can be no widespread evangelization of England unless the work is undertaken by the lay people of the Church. . . . The main duty of the clergy must be to train the lay members of the congregation in their work of witness."

WILLIAM TEMPLE.

THE AIM OF EVANGELISM

Conversion. THE aim of evangelism is Conversion. Conversion is the re-orientation of life from self to God through Christ Jesus.

Conversion may be sudden: a revolutionary experience, like a revealing flash of lightning, which enables the convert to commemorate a spiritual birthday. Or conversion may be gradual: an evolutionary development, like the dawn of day, or the miracle of the harvest field.[1] But whether sudden or gradual, it is the birthright of every child of God to be converted, or (in St. Paul's phrase) to "be *alive* unto God in Jesus Christ our Lord."[2] Short of this there is no stopping place for the evangelist, no sure resting place for the convert.

Its meaning. 79   The act of conversion is the personal acceptance of Christ Jesus as Saviour and King. In the *Retrospect* of his life Bishop Hensley Henson recalls how he asked Bishop Linton, "the most successful evangelist of Moslems that our Church possesses . . . what he found to be the element in Christianity which appealed most to the Mohammedans in Persia." The answer was that "it was the Person and Character of Christ, *not* conviction of sin. The sense of sin developed in converts, but it played no part in their conversion." Bishop Linton finds the same equally true in Birmingham.

As regards the old life, conversion is the removal of the effects of sin, for sin (as we have seen) consists in the centring of man upon himself, instead of upon God.

1 Mark iv, 26-29.
2 Rom. vi, 11.

As regards the new life, conversion is a changed heart, which results in a surrendered will and, eventually, in transformed desire.

80   It is unfortunate that, generally speaking, "the idea of **Its meaning** conversion is misconceived, and its importance under-estimated."[3] **miscon-** **ceived.** We quote one reason that has been given: "In a country like this, which has been Christian at least in name for many centuries, it had come to be supposed that every normal person was brought up in a Christian home, and therefore became a Christian as a matter of course, and so did not need to be *converted* to Christianity. Under these conditions, the word *conversion* came to be reserved for the comparatively eccentric people who made a dramatic change of faith, who became Roman Catholics, for instance; or for notorious evil livers, such as burglars, who joined the Salvation Army! Anyhow, it had come to be assumed, until recent times, that conversion was an unusual type of experience which did not occur, and did not need to occur, in the lives of normal and sensible Christians, such as members of the Church of England generally supposed themselves to be."[3]

81   We cannot expect to get far with evangelism until three **Its necessity** facts are faced. First, the vast majority of English people need to **for** **evangelists.** be converted to Christianity. Secondly, a large number of Church people also require to be converted, in the sense of their possessing that personal knowledge of Christ which can be ours only by the dedication of the whole self, whatever the cost. Thirdly, such personal knowledge of Christ is the only satisfactory basis for testimony to others.

It will thus be realised that the really daunting feature of modern evangelism is not the masses of the population to be converted, but that most of the worshipping community are only half-converted. The aim of evangelism must be to appeal to all, within as well as without the Church, for that decision for Christ which shall make the state of salvation we call conversion the usual experience of the normal Christian.

THE TWO STAGES IN EVANGELISM

82   Conversion, as the sole aim of all evangelistic effort, must **Two stages** always be kept clearly in mind by the evangelist. In the process **in evan-** **gelism.** we may distinguish two stages which, though logically successive, are generally intertwined in practice.

---

3 Rev. A. Vidler: *God's demand and Man's response*, p. 78.

1. Preparation for the Gospel.

83 The first or preliminary stage consists in arousing the interest of those to whom the message is being delivered—meeting their objections and intellectual difficulties, and showing how the Gospel finds men just where they are, satisfying their deepest needs. We shall devote a subsequent chapter to this aspect of evangelism.[4]

2. Presenting the Gospel.

84 The other stage is the actual bringing of the convert to the point of decision—that personal abandonment to the Divine will and purpose which is involved in the acceptance of Christ Jesus as Saviour and King.

This is primarily a matter of the individual will. While, therefore, all evangelism is in essence a personal ministry, this is more markedly so in the second stage of evangelism. For the effecting of a conversion, under the operation of the Holy Spirit, the direct and immediate contact of a person with a person almost always seems to be called for.

PERSONAL TESTIMONY IN EVANGELISM

Personal Testimony,

85 If we are to confront men and women with God, the proclamation of the Gospel must be endorsed by our own personal testimony to its converting assurance and power. Evangelists "must be able to speak out of a genuine experience of what Jesus Himself means to them. . . . In the end that is the only means of an effective evangelism."[5]

by lip

Such personal testimony is of two kinds—by lip and by life. Neither is truly effective without the other, and both are an inescapable Christian duty. Yet both invite the temptation to self-advertisement and incur the accusation of self-glorification. "The banner of the Gospel must be upheld by personal testimony, but its bearer must be lost in its folds.[6]

and by life.

The testimony of our lives to the saving power of Christ is quite obviously essential in order to confirm the testimony of our lips. In the witnessing Christian all the wholesome natural virtues will be seen to be alive, but transfigured through the orientation from self to God in Christ. Indeed, a life lived in the world, and yet not of the world, is itself witness of the highest order. It is what H. M. Stanley described as a "sermon acted," as he saw it in the daily life of David Livingstone.[7]

4 See Chap. v.
5 Dr. William Temple, Church Army Sermon Westminster Abbey, 3rd Nov 1942.
6 Dr. F. J. Chavasse.
7 "He preached no sermon by word of mouth while I was in company with him, but each day of my companionship with him saw a sermon acted."

But it is insufficiently understood that, however compelling may be the attractive power of a holy life, there is still the need for a word of interpretation which explains that life and unites it with the Christ Who is its source.[8]

86   In such personal testimony we draw a clear distinction, all **Witness and preaching.** through this Report, between the obligation to *witness*, and the vocation to *preach the Gospel*.

Personal witness, the natural speaking to others about Christ, is incumbent on all Christians, and commanded as a duty by the Ascended Head of the Church Himself.[9]

To preach the Gospel[10] includes, also, that public telling forth for which many witnesses are more specially gifted[11] and to which they are more particularly called.[12] Evangelism includes both personal witness and Gospel preaching. Who, then, are called to exercise this personal ministry which St. Paul describes as that of ambassadors of the word of reconciliation?[13]

87   In His final charge to His disciples before His ascension, **The Apostolate of the whole Church.** the Risen Christ declared: "Ye shall receive power when the Holy Ghost is come upon you: and ye shall be my witnesses."[9] Thereby we are taught (what the whole of the New Testament enforces) that "the primary purpose for which the Spirit is given is that we may bear witness to Christ. We must not expect the gift while we ignore the purpose. A Church which ceases to be missionary will not be, and cannot rightly expect to be, 'spiritual.'"[14]

The charge of Christ at His ascension and the subsequent gift of the Holy Spirit were not confined to the twelve apostles, an ordained ministry, but were given to all the members of the infant Church. Thus, upon the *whole* Church of Christ, clergy and laity alike, the duty to witness is equally laid, and the power to witness is equally bestowed. The only difference is that the peculiar responsibility rests upon the clergy of inspiring, training and directing the evangelistic body. We are thus brought face to face with the truth which has been so disastrously obscured in recent years, both in the thought and practice of the Church. It is that:—

8 II Cor: iv, 5.
9 Acts i, 8.
10 Mark xvi, 15.
11 I Cor: 12, 1-11.
12 Gal: i, 15, 16.
13 II Cor: v, 20.
14 Dr. William Temple: *Readings in St. John*, p. 386.

The ministry of evangelism is a charge laid upon the whole Church by its Lord. It is the very essence of the Christian calling.

Clergy and people, waiting upon God, must plan together, and work together, to recover in practice the Apostolate of the whole Church, and thus to fashion the Church itself into Christ's weapon for evangelism.

THE PART OF THE CLERGY IN EVANGELISM

The Parish Priest. IF the Apostolate of the whole Church, clergy and laity alike, is to be recovered, if the Church itself is to become a weapon for evangelism, the clergy are, and must be, the key to the situation.

The spiritual temperature of a congregation depends chiefly on the parish priest. That awful responsibility is his, and he cannot escape from it. Generally speaking the Church cannot rise higher than the lives of its clergy. The parish priest must, also, himself exercise a converting ministry, charged as he is at his ordination "to seek for Christ's sheep that are dispersed abroad." Above all, the parish priest is the gift of the Ascended Christ to the Church "in order fully to equip His people for the work of serving—for the building up of Christ's body." [15] He must make time for the study and prayer that is necessary if he is to train the people in the pews, and send them out as witnesses for Christ.

In any recovery of the Apostolate of the whole Church, the clergy themselves will be the first to affirm that they need (1) a fresh vision of God, (2) a new sense of expectation in their ministry, and (3) relief from heavy routine duty in order to "continue steadfastly in prayer and in the ministry of the Word." [16]

1. A FRESH VISION OF GOD

'The spirit of heaviness.' *89*   Up to the present, those called to the ministry of the Church have been trained with a pastoral, rather than an evangelistic, office in view. The assumption that the Church is conterminous with the nation, upon which parochial organization is based, seems to per-

15 Eph. iv, 12 (Dr. Weymouth's translation).
16 Acts vi, 4.

sist though it is no longer true. Here is a chief cause for that sense of frustration which is afflicting so many of the clergy with a haunting sense of inadequacy. Nor is it surprising that, emmeshed in such a system, a spiritual apathy has settled upon many of them. Confronted with a task that was often humanly impossible, frequently burdened with domestic anxiety and generally left to themselves in lonely isolation, it is only surprising that so many have not succumbed. For such a situation the paramount necessity is that the parish clergy as a body should gain a new vision, fresh hope and a baptism of the Holy Spirit.

90 Any forward move, therefore, in evangelism must begin with the clergy themselves, and with their coming together to gain a new liberation into the vision of the glory of God. Our first recommendation as a Commission is that the Bishops (if they have not already done so) should arrange for gatherings of their clergy for this purpose. Where such conventions have been held, the gratitude of the clergy who have shared in them has been most moving, and the outcome has been the transfiguration of many a subsequent ministry. **Conventions for the clergy.**

2. An Evangelistic Ministry

91 Possessed of a new hope in God's power and purpose, the parochial clergy will be enabled to look upon their ministry with new eyes, seeing the parish as a sphere for evangelism, and themselves as called to be fishers of men. **Parochial evangelism.**

A converting ministry does not necessarily mean special efforts or a specialised ministry; though the employment of both have, from time to time, proved eminently successful. A converting ministry implies an attitude of expectancy which pervades and influences every department of an ordinary parochial ministry. Each individual is seen as one for whom Christ died, and Church services and parochial organizations as the appointed means of presenting Christ more clearly as Saviour, Lord and King.

We have already seen how personal is the actual work of evangelism—the direct appeal to individuals to yield their hearts and lives to the sovereignty of Christ. For this reason the parish priest, with his daily and intimate contacts with all and sundry, is presented with the most splendid field for evangelism, if only he can view the parochial routine with *expectancy,* and use the

Occasional Offices of the Church as a personal appeal to God's children at the most responsive moments in their lives.

Church Services. 92   Though the phrase "the non-worshipping members of the community" shows that ordinary *Church Services* no longer afford a point of contact between the parish priest and his parishioners, yet seekers after truth continually explore the possibilities of public worship; nor can we forget that a large proportion of regular worshippers are only half-converted.

Seeing that the vast majority of the population has no understanding of liturgical worship, there will be the need, on occasion or for short periods, of informal services to which non-worshippers can be invited, introduced to the art of worship, and instructed in it. But the regular services of the Church can also proclaim the evangel even to those unversed in their use, if they are made intelligible and given coherence round a theme.

Moreover, the reality of public worship, while yet not understood, can confront even the casual visitor with the Presence of God, if it is infused with the warmth of fellowship and filled with the atmosphere of true adoration.[17] This can only happen when clergy, church officials, and the general congregation all conspire together to bring each their own particular and essential contribution to the make-up of the whole. But a co-operating congregation cannot come into being apart from the inspiration of the commissioned leader of divine worship. The popular notion thus remains true that "for all practical purposes the Church is its liturgy and its parsons. The God it offers to the world is the God revealed in its services and its sermons."[18]

Preaching. 93   The decrying of *Preaching*, which became fashionable in some quarters during the present century, has constituted a fatal departure from the past tradition of the whole Church.

In the works of both Franciscan and Dominican writers, the surprising assertion is found that: "It is more profitable to hear God's word in preaching than to hear mass."[19] Preaching was termed a sacrament by Bishop Nicholas Ridley, "to whose sermons the people resorted, swarming round him like bees." The

---

17 See also pars. 313, 319, 320.

18 St. Martin's Review, May, 1941.

19 Quoted by Canon C. Smyth: *The Art of Preaching*, pp. 15, 16. Cf. St. Bernadine of Sienna (1380-1444): "And if of these two things you can do only one—either hear the mass or hear the sermon—you should let the mass go, rather than the sermon. . . . There is less peril for your soul in not hearing mass than in not hearing the sermon."

Ordinal, with its solemn delivery of the Bible to the priest with the charge: "Take thou authority to preach the Word of God," emphasises his call to the exercise of a prophetic ministry: "Thus saith the Lord."

Here, again, a preaching ministry to have effect requires the co-operation of an expectant and praying congregation. No one has earned the right to criticise the sermon who has not first prayed for the preacher.

Evangelistic sermons are not simply those which call for definite acceptance of Christ as Saviour and Lord, though such appeals might well be more frequent. Every sermon (whether instructional, ethical or homiletical) can be evangelistic in the sense that through it God challenges the hearer's will, and that it demands decision and action. For this, there is a crying need for a return to Bible preaching. Without it there can be no evangelistic ministry in the pulpit; for the Word of God is "living and active," and preaches to the conscience apart from the preacher.

To obtain the full value from preaching, experience has shown the benefit of advertising, from time to time, a discussion after the service on the subject of the sermon. Young people, especially, are attracted by such a practice, and cease to regard the pulpit as a coward's castle.

94   *Visiting* can be a real adventure in evangelism, if it is **Visiting.** undertaken in a spirit of expectancy, and buttressed with prayer. but a house-going parson will not make a church-going people, if his visits mean nothing more than a friendly social call: nothing, certainly, that required the laying on of hands at ordination. With thought and method, too, visits can be paid when they will be most fruitful; for example, on great anniversaries in the lives of the parishioners. Furthermore, whenever a visit meets with a response that seems to promise the hope of a conversion, it should be followed up and prayed over until a decision is reached one way or the other.

95   We turn to the opportunity afforded by the *Occasional* **The Occa-** *Offices.* For this the parish priest must be given relief and help, in **sional** **Offices.** order to preserve spiritual vitality, and to have time for the thought, prayer and pains that are necessary for so constant and exacting a task. Baptism, Confirmation, Marriage, the visiting of the sick and the bereaved, all provide close and lasting points of contact

with people at moments when they are particularly susceptible to spiritual influence. The practical, and increasing, difficulties surrounding them all are only too familiar to faithful parish priests (more particularly to those in charge of large and congested areas), and they form the subject of constant discussion among them.

We feel constrained to draw special attention to the evangelistic opportunities presented by Confirmation and Marriage.

Confirmation. 96   At *Confirmation* (to quote the *Joint Committee on Confirmation*) " the members of the priestly Body of the Great High Priest are consecrated by the Holy Spirit, so that strengthened by the increase of His manifold gifts of grace they may be enabled faithfully to fulfil their ministry of worship and of witness."[20] An essential part of that ministry is the obligation to witness, and Confirmation, from earliest times, has been considered the Ordination of the Laity, when they are commissioned and empowered to exercise their apostleship of evangelism.[21]

This does not necessarily mean that Confirmation must be deferred to mature years. The age of emotional awakening in the early teens is the time when so many children first hear the call of God to witness, and do in fact bear witness.[22] But whether young or old, **no candidate should be presented for Confirmation for whom the laying on of hands does not mean the receiving of the Holy Spirit's power in response to a real decision for Christ, and an honest intention "to serve Him in the fellowship of the Church."** To present candidates with little previous attachment to the Church, solely on the strength of having attended a course of instruction, and with no appeal to the conscience, is to manufacture lapsed communicants.

Marriage. 97   *Marriage* presents the parish priest with, perhaps, the greatest evangelistic opportunity of all. As at no other time in their lives, those who are about to embark on the adventure of uniting their personalities "as joint heirs of the grace of life," and of setting up a home for themselves, are moved to listen to the claims of Christ and to yield their hearts to His obedience. The moment of opportunity soon passes. According to a well-known missioner who has also had wide parochial experience, two months

---

20 *Confirmation To-day* (1944), par. 16.
21 See par. 112.
22 The Bishop of Chelmsford tells how, at a Convention of Missionaries, all present were asked to state when God first called them to the mission field. In the case of 75%, it was before they were 15 years old.

before and after marriage is the "acceptable time." It is generally then or never.

The practice of giving instruction to young couples before their marriage is, happily, on the increase; though many of the clergy would be grateful for further guidance on the matter. We would emphasize that no preparation for marriage is adequate which does not appeal for decision for Christ, as the only sound foundation for married life.

THE TRAINING OF THE CLERGY IN EVANGELISM

98   In view of the immense opportunities open to parochial **The need of** evangelism, it is alarming to discover how few of the clergy have **training.** been given any training in the work of an evangelist, such as in the art of preaching or of personal dealing with enquirers; how few, again, have been used of God to bring a soul to new birth; and how many are embarrassed and tongue-tied when the occasion offers of speaking to individuals about the deepest matters of their eternal welfare.

There is a general need for the clergy to be trained, not only in evangelism, but also how to bring peace to a troubled conscience and to give that "ghostly counsel and advice" for which the Prayer Book takes it for granted that the parish priest is adequately equipped.

We venture to enumerate some of the directions in which we believe the clergy are asking for help. What we have to suggest should certainly form part of the training of all ordination candidates, and also be included in the programme of Schools of Evangelism for the clergy.

99   We are gravely disturbed to discover how many of the **Prayer.** clergy seem to have received inadequate training in prayer and meditation. Great numbers of priests neither know how to pray themselves, still less how to teach the art of true prayer to their people. There is the need of Schools of Prayer for the clergy, and of all the help and encouragement they can possibly be given in this vital matter. We touch here the very heart of successful evangelism. On the one hand, evangelism cannot exist without that vision and power which regular habits of private devotion alone can communicate. On the other hand, it is so very difficult

for the harassed and isolated parish priest to maintain, steadfastly and ardently, the inner life of daily communion with God.

Knowledge and use of the Bible.

100   The ignorance of the Bible to-day, not only in the ranks of the laity but also amongst many of the clergy (and particularly the younger clergy) is really horrifying. Yet there is nothing more vital for the work of evangelism. The Bible contains the title deeds of our Faith. How many priests, to-day, by pointing to passages and verses from the Holy Scriptures, can bring that assurance of salvation to enquirers which our Bible-loving forefathers were able to mediate to countless multitudes? The Comfortable Words in the Holy Communion service show this ministry of the Word in operation. Bishops tell of candidates for ordination who cannot point "to any words of the Lord Jesus Christ where He promises forgiveness of sins to anybody and everybody."[23] The Gospel in Holy Scripture must be a foremost subject in every School of Evangelism.

Understanding of human personality.

101   The Prayer Book expects in parish priests a discretion and learning that qualifies them to give "ghostly counsel and advice," sometimes termed "spiritual direction." A wise understanding of human personality is the foundation of the whole ministry of reconciliation and of absolution, of which priests are supposed to be accredited ambassadors. This personal ministry has always been exacting, but never more so than in our highly neurotic age which is crowding the waiting rooms of psychiatrists, and when great numbers of ordinarily normal people (by ignoring the all-pervasive spiritual element in man) are subjecting themselves to severe emotional stresses and conflicts.

Moral theology and some knowledge of psychology have become increasingly important ingredients in pastoralia. They, must, therefore, occupy a proportionate place in the curriculum at theological colleges and post-ordination schools. Such training is necessary if only that those who have to deal personally with individuals may know when, and to whom, they should refer cases which require more expert treatment. Indeed, we see the need for the formation of central clinics where the combined co-operation of priests, doctors and psychologists would be available.

The art of preaching.

102   The standard of preaching throughout the Church, speaking generally, is deplorably low. The bitter complaints of the laity upon this score are too general and widespread to be dismissed

23 *Evangelism through News Teams*, p. 18.   (Church Army, 1/-.)

lightly. Yet it would be unfair to blame the clergy for their deficiencies in this direction. There is an art in preaching, as in teaching, which does not come by light of nature save to a specially gifted minority. What teacher would feel himself well equipped for his profession if he received no more instruction in his art than is afforded to most preachers?

In this connection the remark of a young flight lieutenant, a lecturer in an R.A.F. training school, made to one of the Archbishop's visitors, is worth quoting. He said: "I have been a lecturer here for over two years, and I enjoy my work very much. A short time ago the R.A.F. started courses for lecturers, and I was sent on one. I did not want to go, and thought it unnecessary and a waste of time. But I had to go, and soon came to see how faulty my technique had been. I am also finding my work more interesting. Have you got anything like that in the Church for the clergy?" Schools of Preaching are required to teach the importance and the content, as well as the art, of the public ministry of the Word.

103 Up to the present, the technique of evangelism has not formed part of what is usually included under pastoralia. It is as necessary, now, for missionaries in Christian England, as it has always been for those who carry the Gospel overseas. Definite instruction in the art and methods of evangelism should be provided by lectures before ordination, and by Schools of Training after ordination. *The technique of evangelism.*

Instruction, however, is not enough. Evangelism can only be learnt by actually seeing it done, and in the doing of it oneself. We strongly recommend that opportunity should be given for all ordination candidates and younger clergy to have practical experience of evangelism, whether through participation in missions or I.C.F. Crusades, or by advantage being taken of the evangelistic campaigns for university students conducted by the Church Army and others. We also suggest that dioceses might, with great profit, extend the practice of holding missions conducted by missioners largely drawn from the diocese itself.

104 The leadership of Discussion Groups is a skilled job, if they are to grip and hold. But it is one which can be acquired from those with experience. Careful attention should be given to the training necessary, for the method of informal discussion will un- *The conduct of discussion groups and cells.*

doubtedly become an increasingly important weapon in the parish priest's armoury.

To know, too, how to act as leader, or priest-adviser, of cells or companies, will also prove of great value and importance in the near future.

3. RELIEF FOR THE CLERGY

The parochial rush.

105   Greatly as the clergy need, and will heartily welcome, such additional aids to their mental and spiritual equipment, it is equally true that they sorely need relief in other directions.

The life of a parish priest in a large town has become a rushing struggle to get through the innumerable tasks which crowd upon him day after day, and to meet incessant unforeseen demands. Besides the exacting round of parochial duty, there is the burden of administrative and clerical work which falls upon him as a trusted public servant, but not as a spiritual pastor.[24] If he does manage to secure an apparently clear hour for reading or study in the morning, the front door bell or telephone may be relied upon to break into it. This is no exaggeration, and the strain goes on week after week and month after month.

Unlike the majority of men, his week-ends bring no slackening of pressure, though Sunday is not necessarily his busiest day. Moreover, the possibility of taking a day off each week is frequently denied him; and, with the increasing shortage of priests, even the annual holiday is becoming increasingly difficult to arrange. In the country the situation is different, but even there the multiplicity of little jobs, including probably the care of an over-large garden, leaves him often with remarkably little time for quiet, for constructive thought and study.

The shortage of clergy.

106   The basic fact is that the parochial clergy are now all too few. They cannot, therefore, get free from the necessary routine duties of a parish in order to give themselves to the absorbing personal and pastoral ministry of evangelising their people. The following figures will give some indication of the proportions of the problem : —

---

24 Would it not be possible for the signatures of accredited lay-workers to be accepted by the civil authorities, where now the signature of a minister of religion is required?

YEAR	POPULATION	CLERGY
*1688	5.5 millions	10,000
1911	34.0 ,,	20,086
1921	35.6 ,,	17,326
1931	37.3 ,,	18,856
1938	38.4 ,,	17,139

* G. M. Trevelyan: *English Social History*, p. 277.

It will be seen that between the two wars, while the population of England increased by four millions, the number of the clergy decreased by three thousand. The shortage has further increased during the present war by nearly another three thousand, and will steadily continue until Service candidates for ordination have been demobilised and trained.

107 During this acute post-war shortage the temptation will be for the laity to demand, and the Bishops to allow, a lower standard of training and of personal qualification, in order to save parish priests from breaking down under an impossible strain. We are convinced that were the Church to succumb, and to lower instead of raising the ordination standard, fatal and far reaching damage would be done to the cause of true religion: above all, to the cause nearest to our Saviour's heart—evangelism. *Keeping up the standard.*

At the same time, revolutionary thinking and action alone will enable the relatively small army of parish priests to exercise themselves an evangelistic ministry, to train the laity for their work of witness and of preaching the Gospel, and to gain that quiet for thought, study, and the nurturing of their own inner life which are so essential whether for the evangelist or the trainer of evangelists. How is the necessary relief to be given?

108 The situation should force the Church to answer the question whether it could not "by a fuller and more intelligent use of women, strengthen and supplement the ministry of men in its service, and also enable them to make their special contribution."[25] *The recruiting of women,*

109 There is, too, the obvious remedy of recruiting the ranks of Church Army captains and sisters who have so splendidly proved *and of lay ministries.*

[25] Report of the Archbishop's Committee (1944) on *Women's Work in the Church*, par. 4.

E

their worth; as also for the better training and wider use of Readers who might, for example, be more used for preaching, even when a priest is present at the service.

Bishops' messengers. *110* We would also advocate the advisability of reviving and extending the idea of Bishops' Messengers, which came into being entirely through lay initiative during the last war. Bands of such women messengers are still operating in some dioceses. Bishops' messengers should include men, and become a diocesan force for evangelism, acting as the representatives of the Bishop under his authority.

The Apostolate of the laity. *111* But if the seventeen thousand priests of the Church of England are to become seventeen thousand evangelists and trainers of evangelists, something far more revolutionary is demanded than the strengthening of auxiliary ministries open to faithful Churchmen and Churchwomen—nothing less, indeed, than the full co-operation of the whole body of the laity in the Apostolate of the Church. We pass, therefore, to consider the part the laity are called on to play in the work of evangelism, and their training for their apostolate.

THE PART OF THE LAITY IN EVANGELISM

Essential for evangelism. THE inalienable right and duty of the laity to take its full part in the spiritual work of the Church, finds forceful expression all down the Church's history.

In the New Testament St. Peter calls Church-people "an elect race, a royal priesthood, a holy nation, a people for God's own possession."[26] As such the early Church made full use both of its laymen and women: "The most numerous and successful missionaries of the Christian religion were not the regular teachers but Christians themselves, by dint of their loyalty and courage . . . We cannot hesitate to believe that the very great mission of Christianity was in reality accomplished by means of informal missionaries."[27]

In the fourth century, Jerome described Confirmation as the ordination of the laity.[28] Thomas Aquinas (1226-1274) likewise

26 I Pet: ii, 9. In the Greek Bible "laos" first means "the people" as distinguished from the priests, and then "The People of God."
27 Harnack: Expansion of Christianity, vol. i, pp. 458-460.
28 "Sacerdotium laici, id est Baptisma" (then not separated from Confirmation). *Contra Lucifer* 4.

taught that at Confirmation the layman was given "through the Holy Spirit, power and responsibility, not only to effect his own salvation, but also by sharing in the priesthood of Christ to act as *His Apostle in the salvation of the world.*"[29]

An apostle is one who is sent. We would stress the Thomist doctrine of the Apostleship of the Laity. Everyone of the laity is commissioned and empowered at Confirmation for the apostleship of witness. Some of the laity are called for the apostleship of preaching the Gospel.

The Reformation re-established the right of the laity to the "priesthood of all believers." The nineteenth century is a remarkble record of the spiritual achievements of the laity in politics and social reform, in philanthropy and education, in missions overseas and evangelism at home. But speaking generally the Church of our generation, both in its thinking and practice, has departed from God's ordained means of extending His Kingdom. The result, as ever, has been failure and frustration.

It is not, therefore, as a matter of expediency that we put the mobilisation of the laity for the work of evangelism in the very forefront of our Recommendations. It is a matter of simple obedience to a Divine command.[30]

113 The practice of a layman taking a direct part in evangelistic work is not something unknown in our day. Apart from those lay men and women who are employed either as part-time or whole-time church workers, there have always been special occasions (such as preparation for a parochial mission) when, in a well-run parish, lay co-operation with the clergy has reached a high level. What would strike the average layman as novel would be the idea of evangelism being a *normal* Christian duty; or that any real responsibility in the matter rests upon the layman himself. *The laity and church work.*

What, then, are the objections which are likely to spring to the mind of the average layman when confronted by the challenge to take his full and rightful part in evangelism? Usually they are pre-occupation and reticence.

114 The objection, "I have not the time to give," is of modern currency. Before the 1914 war the principle (if not universally recognised) largely obtained of every keen communicant under- *Pre-occupation.*

29 *The Ministry and the Sacraments*, p. 60. S.C.M., 1937.
30 See par. 87.

taking some kind of church work—Sunday School and Bible Class teaching, district visiting, club and youth-organization leadership.[31]   With the increase of leisure and of opportunities for entertainment, such posts have become more difficult to fill; and the shirking of duty has been greatest among those who have had most leisure to enjoy.

On the other hand, these war years have proved to what extent, even in times of greatest stress, men and women can, and will, undertake extra duties if they feel the cause to be sufficiently urgent.   The splendid devotion of the civilian population, and their newly found fellowship in every form of voluntary national employment, shows what resources of service might be enlisted for building up the fellowship of the church in every parish.

In any case, the excuse "I have no time" cannot be pleaded where evangelism is concerned.   Evangelism is not a part-time, but a full-time, obligation; and it is exercised at home, at work and in society, rather than in specifically church organizations. Generally the plea of pre-occupation is a cloak for the real objection, which is shyness in speaking about the things of God.

Reticence.   *115*   This shyness, deep rooted in the natural reserve of the English temperament, is not without its value.   It is a safeguard against the glibness which repels, and ensures that the testimony of the lips shall not outrun the reality of conviction.

As we have seen, personal witness to Christ must always be two-fold in character: a life that reflects the love of Christ in human affairs, and spoken testimony to Him as Saviour and King.   The one must interpret the other.   It is, therefore, the duty of all Christians to overcome their natural shrinking when occasion offers for the spoken word of testimony.

Admiral Sir John Tovey has, on two occasions, well expressed the moral struggle involved: "It is a terrible pity we are so shy in talking about religion. . . . As a result of my mother's teaching, I have always had a great faith in God, and a firm belief in the efficacy of prayer.   Some twelve years ago I longed to say something to my ship's company to try to help the young men in their belief and practice of prayer.   But for a long time I funked it, and had to summon up all my moral courage before I succeeded." And again: "Why is it that we are so painfully shy of talking about

---

[31] "Of three successive Lord Chancellors, Lords Cairns (1819-1885), Hatherley (1801-1881) and Selborne (1812-1895), each taught in a Sunday School nearly all his life.   (R. C. K. Ensor: *England 1870-1914*, p. 139, footnote.)

religion? It would seem that we are almost ashamed of admitting openly that we are Christians . . . I admit myself that even up to now it has always required all my courage to talk to my ship's company about religion."

We cannot exaggerate the importance of breaking down this traditional English reserve which produces a Church of "silent saints." As Prebendary Wilson Carlile (who coined this phrase) declared: "I have got the biggest job I have ever tackled in my life. I am trying to open the mouths of the people in the pews."

116 The Christian obligation of spoken witness does not require **Personal** from all the duty of addressing public audiences: still less of button- **witness,** holing comparative strangers. It does demand being able to give a reason for the faith that is in us, when asked by a friend; and of praying that such openings shall be given and used by us. Neither, for spoken testimony, is autobiography necessary; though, when used with restraint, and with the steadfast object of preaching "not ourselves, but Christ Jesus,"[32] there is no disguising its telling effect or that it has been mightily used of God.

The essential matter is that testimony to Christ shall be given, and that it should be from first hand personal experience. An affirmation that rests on hearsay, or on authority, is ruled out of court as evidence. The good news of the Gospel will carry conviction in proportion as it is the outcome of our personal knowledge of the reality and power of the living Christ. The non-worshipping members of the community are not impressed by a message based on the authority of the Church, unless it is supported by the first hand testimony of the messenger.

117 How are we to help the ordinary layman to overcome this **liberated by** shyness, which is so largely reducing the value of the witness of **fellowship,** his life?

We believe that ordinary Christians may be helped to talk naturally and openly about Christ if they do not regard themselves as isolated prophets, but as representatives of the evangelising Church, and as the tongue of the Body of Christ. That "fellowship in the Gospel," of which St. Paul and his converts were so conscious, must become a more real and living experience to Church-people.

To this end, membership in an Evangelistic Group or News Team has proved of the greatest value. Not only do such make an

32 II Cor: iv. 5.

effective impact upon the outside world, but they effectually liber-
ate their own members from the domination of that "dumb devil"
which so often enchains sincere Christians.

**and the
road to
faith.**
118   Often, however, there is a deeper reason than self-consciousness for the shyness that fetters utterance. It arises from a notion,
on the part of the would-be evangelist, that he has not the right to
speak, since he lacks that assurance of faith which he would
fain possess but cannot feel.   There is here a confusion of thought,
which equates faith with feeling.

The fact that we desire to witness to Christ is itself evidence
of the presence of faith within us: "When a soul desires God, it
already possesses Him."   But more than this, St. Paul's statement, "With the heart man believeth unto righteousness; and with
the mouth confession is made unto salvation,"[33] endorses the
common experience that intellectual assent to the truth of Christ,
becomes personal trust in Christ, through spoken testimony—it may
be to one friend. It must always be remembered that the evangelist
is not required to come to the enquirer *de haut en bas,* as one who
is satisfied that he has achieved. Rather he comes as a fellow-seeker
who is still seeking, but has good reason to believe that he has found
the Way.

THE TRAINING OF THE LAITY IN EVANGELISM

**An urgent
task.**
119   How then are the laity to be mobilised and trained for the
work of evangelism?   The chief obstacle (as we have seen) is that
so many church people are only half-converted.[34] But, clearly, it is
impossible to wait till the whole of the Church shall be wholly
converted.   On the contrary, it is by engaging in evangelism that
the whole Church will be revived and its ardour fanned into flame.

For example, in the Indian diocese of Dornakal, something
like three-quarters of the entire communicant membership of the
Church takes part in an annual week of witness to their Hindu
fellow-countrymen, giving up work and pay for this purpose.
Though the week's campaign has been responsible for a rapid expansion of Christianity in South India, the late Bishop Azariah
stressed its importance, even more, because of the emergence
thereby among the witnesses themselves of a higher quality both
of devotion and consistency of life.   The mobilisation and the
training of the laity must be begun at once, and resolutely pursued
step by step.

---

33 Rom. x, 10.   34 See par. 81.

120 We have urged that the first step towards the evangelising of England must be a call to the clergy to renewal. One purpose of such renewal would be that the clergy may equip themselves to train the laity, without whose full co-operation the task cannot be accomplished. The mobilisation of the laity.

The next step would generally be the summoning, by the clergy, of their Parochial Church Councils to review the position and to plan for action. It is "the primary duty of the Council in every parish to co-operate with the Incumbent in the initiation, conduct and development of Church work both within the parish and without."[35] This chief function of the Parochial Church Council is often overlooked, or crowded out by other business. Thus to place upon Church Councils the responsibility for evangelising the parish, would effect an evangelistic work upon the members themselves. At the same time, some of the congregation most ready to help will not be on the Council, and their mobilisation should also be effected.

121 We, therefore, suggest to Parochial Church Councils that they should consider the holding of a Convention in each parish, or in groups of parishes, for the deepening of the spiritual life, and for instruction in the faith and in prayer. It must be remembered that the Church is at present itself a field for evangelism rather than a force for evangelism. 1. Conventions for church people.

122 The purposed outcome of such Conventions for church congregations would be offers of service for evangelism, whether by witness or by preaching the Gospel. It may well be that previous calls to renewal have failed to achieve their hopes because they lacked this constructive purpose. Volunteers should be formed into groups with the object (like the Apostles) of making themselves effective witnesses to Christ. 2. Evangelistic companies or cells.

We emphasise elsewhere the importance of the cell, or group, method.[36] It is, perhaps, the most effective instrument for evangelism under modern conditions. At the moment we see in it the best means of training for witness, as the members meet for prayer, for Bible study, to "provoke one another unto love and good works,"[37] to wait on the guidance of the Holy Spirit, to experience His promised outpouring on steadfast fellowship, and to plan evangelistic advance.

---

[35] The Parochial Church Councils (Powers) Measure, 1921, Sect. 2.
[36] See pars. 149-155 and 299.
[37] Heb. x, 24.

3. Training Schools.

123   We have been impressed by reports of the success of Confirmation Schools and Moral Leadership Courses, arranged for the Forces by Chaplains' Departments. At these schools officers and men have received instruction in Christian living and witness for a period of five or six days. Before the war, similar experiments in the training of the "lay apostolate" amply proved their usefulness. Such schools will be essential for any forward move in evangelism by the Church. They can take the form either of a long week-end, or else of a series of meetings on one evening each week for five or six weeks. They can be arranged on a parochial, or on an area, or on a diocesan basis; and their organisation should be a diocesan responsibility.

4. Teams of Witness.

124   As we have previously stated, the work of evangelism can only be learned by actual practical experience. Out of Training Schools should arise parochial teams of witness, after the pattern of the News Teams already organised by the Church Army.

We cannot do better than commend the idea in the words of the late Archbishop William Temple: "Why should not a team of witness go from one parish to another to join in a campaign of witness, just as they go to play cricket or football? They would need to be coached; so do the cricketers. The clergy who cannot deliver the testimony themselves, except on rare occasions, could often find time to coach them. The young could be trained and sent out; and what a torrent of spiritual eagerness might be released. . . . It does very little harm if an eager layman talks heresy, provided he shows and imparts a love for the Lord Jesus. It does great harm if a priest talks orthodoxy so as to make men think the Gospel is dull or irrelevant. How many of our communicants are in fact missionaries in their own parishes? We must turn our congregations into teams of evangelists."[38]

5. Schools for Leaders.

125   From evangelistic companies, training schools and teams of witness, there will emerge potential leaders, capable of becoming specialists in evangelism. A demand may thus easily arise for more elaborate and prolonged facilities for training than diocesan Schools for Leaders can supply. It would, however, be inadvisable to make any detailed suggestion at the moment. Should the need arise, as we profoundly hope it will, the Council for Evangelism,

[38] *Evangelism through News Teams*: Church Army publication, Marble Arch, W.1. See also pars. 153 and 169.

which we recommend,[39] will be in a position to plan the necessary provision.

126   We do not forget that there will be many who will not be **6. Correspondence courses.** able to take advantage of the means of training which we have outlined. For such, and sometimes as supplementary to other training, we advocate facilities for correspondence training courses. Bible study courses by correspondence are already organised most successfully by the Church Missionary Society. Correspondence training courses in evangelism, which would include instruction in the Faith and teaching on prayer, should be one responsibility of the centre for evangelism we recommend.

127   Finally, we would urge the importance (even as we have **7. Other training.** pressed in the case of candidates for ordination) of instruction in evangelism forming part of the curriculum in all Church training institutions. We are thinking of those established for Deaconesses, Teachers, Moral Welfare Workers, Youth Leaders and the like. Such key people should, also, be specially remembered in the organising of the training schools we have in mind.

THE SCOPE OF LAY EVANGELISM

128   It is obvious that the full participation of the laity in evan- **The use of the laity.** gelism will enormously increase the range of the Church's activity, as well as its efficiency. Not infrequently the laity make better evangelists than the clergy. In every congregation witnesses, and even potential evangelists, are to hand, but they need to be discerned and trained. Neither prophetic nor evangelistic gifts are dependent upon the grace of Orders. At the moment the Church is not using those whom the Holy Ghost has separated from their mother's womb and called for the work.[40]

129   The laity have both wider and also more intimate contacts **Their opportunities for evangelism.** than the clergy with non-worshipping members of the community. They can demonstrate the practical working of Christianity in the home, at their work, and in all their social relationships. With the laity the opportunity of effective witness by life and by lip is constantly present. "Christianity is suffering from the lack of personal recommendation."[41] In many cases, too, the witness of the laity carries greater weight with those outside the churches, and is more

39 See Recommendation, par. 363.
40 Isaiah xlix, 1; Jeremiah i, 5; Acts xiii, 2; and Gal. i, 15.
41 *The Evangelistic Work of the Church* (1918), p. 6.

readily accepted by them than that of the "professional" clergy whose obvious interest it is to get people to church.

The laity essential for evangelism.   *130*   As we have seen, the clergy are far too few to do more than touch the fringe of the problem of evangelising the whole country. It is only possible for the Gospel to reach the whole population through the active co-operation of all church people.

We are convinced that England will never be converted until the laity use the opportunities for evangelism daily afforded by their various professions, crafts and occupations.

Evangelism in the home.   *131*   First and foremost among the crafts is that of home-making, a creation towards which *all* members of the family must contribute their share.

The Christian family has been defined as "a community of persons, with reference beyond itself to the civil order of society on the one hand, and to the Divine society of the Church on the other."[42] As such the family provides the first cell of truly social living—political, cultural and religious. Thus, a self-regarding family, which is thought of solely as an end in itself and is unmindful of duties to neighbourhood, community, Church and State, "may be a breeding-ground of arrant selfishness and anti-social tendencies."[42]

Egotism in personal relationships destroys home-life and poisons community at its very fount. But egotism is, at root, that original sin which refuses to acknowledge God as the universal Father. It is, therefore, the first responsibility of those who, in Christ, have escaped from the sterile circle of self, to consecrate their natural affections to the development of true and fuller personality in the community life of their own homes.[42] .

Family Prayer.   *132*   In this context of home-making, the importance will be recognised of recovering the practice of the family uniting in prayer. Where the father is priest in his own household, the recognition of God as the "Father from whom every family in heaven and on earth derives its name and nature"[43] enriches both personal relationships and the worship of the Church. Where there is no such act of family worship, religion becomes an outside matter of teaching at school and of Sunday worship at Church—

---

[42] See *Home and Family Life*, especially pages 36, 39, 43, 46. (Published for the British Council of Churches, S.C.M. Press. Price 1/-).
[43] Ephesians iii, 15. (Moffatt)

that is, something away from the vivid centre of home, and other than ordinary daily life.

In these days of the morning rush to work and of evening engagements, the regular conduct of daily family worship has undoubtedly become extremely difficult. But in very many cases it would be possible to set apart for the purpose a few moments either before or after the Nine o'clock News. Most families, too, could unite in corporate prayer once a week, on Sundays, it might be before or after tea, or the last thing at night. In any case the practice of Grace before meals can be revived, and include both the asking of a blessing upon the home and the dedication of the home to God's service.

Much has been accomplished towards introducing the practice of family prayer, where the parish priest has not only distributed cards of simple prayers to householders, but has visited the home and taken the prayers himself for the first time.

133   Intimately connected with home religion is the once almost **Bible read-** universal practice of daily Bible reading. It is impossible to **ing and** exaggerate the effect on character of the continual play of God's **study.** Word upon the human mind, when the Bible is thus read daily. There can be little hope of religious revival until the English become once again "the people of a book, and that book the Bible." Indeed, history is the proof that every new movement of spiritual renewal has invariably resulted from a fresh discovery of the Word of God.

Our generation has at its disposal a greater understanding of the Bible than that possessed in any previous age. The searching and scientific study to which the Bible has been subjected during the present century has resulted in the vindication, not the destruction, of its authority. In the words of the Regius Professor of Divinity at Oxford: "Thanks to half a century or so of devoted labours by the scholars known as 'higher critics,' it is possible to read the Bible as the bearer of God's Word to man, without having to subordinate the intelligence of the head to the promptings of the heart."[44] The result is that we possess the very best books that have ever been published to guide the student of the Bible. Their teaching and conclusions should be made available to the public in popular form.

The traditional *format*, too, of the Holy Bible should not, as at present, be such as to discourage the tentative reader. Whatever

44 Canon Leonard Hodgson, D.D., in a broadcast address, Aug. 6th, 1944.

the undoubted technical difficulties, a serious effort is long overdue to give this best seller to the people at a moderate price and in an attractive form.[45] The privileged Presses have a high responsibility in the matter, as also the opportunity of rendering evangelism the most signal service.

Progress is undoubtedly being made in Bible reading and study,[46] but the process requires to be accelerated by persistent effort. The position can only be regarded with grave disquiet so long as many ordination candidates know their Bibles less well than most educated children fifty years ago, or while congregations are mystified by Scriptural allusions such as abounded in any ordinary English book,[47] journal or newspaper from 1611 [48] to the last war.

Local Education Authorities can give notable assistance in building up a Bible loving people, by seeing that children possess a *tidy* Bible while at school, and on leaving are presented with a copy of their own.

Evangelism in the working world. 134   Next in importance to home evangelism is the bearing of testimony to Christ at work. Kipling's *Mulholland's Contract* is the modern version of our Lord's injunction to the healed demoniac, forbidden discipleship and sent instead to be a missionary among his own people. Mulholland tells us how he was converted during a storm at sea, while working on a cattle-boat:—

"An' by the terms of the Contract, as I have read the same,
If He got me to port alive I would exalt His Name
An' praise His Holy Majesty till further orders came."

The further orders were: "back you go to the cattle-boats an' preach My Gospel there." Our sympathy goes out to Mulholland as he obeyed and points us to our own duty:—

"I didn't want to do it, for I knew what I should get,
An' I wanted to preach Religion, handsome an' out of the wet,
But the Word of the Lord were lain on me, an' I done what I
was set."[49]

45 *The Bible Designed to be Read as Literature* (Heinmann. 12/6), and *The Bible for To-day* (Ox. Univ. Press. 21/-) are quite admirable publications in their "set out" and captions, and have discovered the Bible to many. But the prices are prohibitive for Tyndale's "boy that driveth the plough."
46 The circulation of the notes of *The Bible Reading Fellowship* (171 Victoria Street, S.W.1) is 330,000 copies a month, an increase of 90,000 during the war years. *The Scripture Union* (C.S.S.M. House, 5 Wigmore Street, W.1) has approximately a million members in different parts of the world. Half the number are in the British Isles, of whom three-quarters are Church of England.
47 Robert Browning's *Ring and the Book* contains 500 Biblical allusions.
48 The publication of the Authorised Version.
49 *The Seven Seas.*

135   Evangelism in the working world means more than bearing **The Christian and the Economic Order.** personal testimony to Christ in the attempt to present Him to "the man next to one at the bench." It also means claiming for Christ the whole of the particular occupation in which we are engaged, and the doing of our work to reflect His likeness. "One of the tasks laid upon the Church, which is not easy to carry out in the existing state of things, is to re-establish in the experience of men and women a unity of work and worship."[50] In the past, to extend God's Kingdom, has tended to be limited to the bringing of more individuals into it. It also includes the bringing of our every activity, and our performance of it, into harmony with God's sovereign law as revealed by Christ.

136   This involves, as *The Oxford Conference on Church, Community and State* pointed out,[50] a two-fold Christian witness. **Changing the Economic Order.**
First, there is the continual witness to Christ's law of love as the criterion which governs all human relationships, not excepting those of the economic order of society. "Christians have a particular responsibility to make whatever contribution they can towards the transformation, and if necessary the thorough reconstruction, of the present economic and political system, through their membership of political parties, trade unions, employers' organisations, and other groups. In this part of their Christian duty the same characteristics are called for, though in a different form, as those which Christians are called on to show in all their other activities: readiness to make sacrifices, to take effective action, to forgive those that trespass against them, and to love those that seem to be their enemies.[50]

137   There is, also, the other, and complementary Christian witness, of acting like Christ in the economic order as it now exists. **Action within the existing Economic Order.** "Christians are under constraint to carry their faith and loyalty into concrete situations, the daily business and the personal relationships of their life. In the integrity and faithfulness which they bring to 'the daily round and common task' they may be instruments, in some measure, of the creative work and the justice and mercy of God."[50]

138   This being so, the Christian laity should be recognised as **The Priesthood of the laity.** the priesthood of the Church in the working world, and as the Church militant in action in the mission fields of politics, industry and commerce.

50 *The Churches Survey their Task* (1937), pp. 127-129.

The member of Parliament, the town councillor, the employer of labour, the trades' union official, the clerk, the artisan, the farmer and the labourer, should be called on to address Church gatherings on "my job" as naturally as are missionaries on furlough.

Such Christian soldiers and servants, too, should be as naturally remembered in the public worship of the Church as those who throughout the war have been fighting their country's battles.

Thereby the vision of Church people would be enlarged as to the nature of the Church and its operations. Thereby there would cease to be this "discontinuity between the sanctuary and the life and work in office, factory, or home."[51] Thereby the hands of those would be strengthened who in their vocation and ministry seek truly to serve God and extend His Kingdom.

The recognition of the priesthood of the laity is the solution of the problem of evangelising every department of the working world. To strengthen its witness in industry, the development of Factory Chaplains is to be fostered; and it is encouraging to find how often parish priests in the neighbourhood prove themselves well qualified for the responsible post. The further question of priests working in factories, or of workers in factories being ordained priests, raises so many problems that we do not feel competent to pronounce upon it. We append as a note to this chapter the report of the important *ad hoc* committee convened to go into the matter, and commend it to the attention of the Council for Evangelism we advocate.[52]

Evangelism in special vocations
139 Once the universal obligation to evangelise is recognised, it will be seen that certain (and often unsuspected) vocations offer peculiar opportunities for evangelism, and are indeed key posts for Christian influence.

The Teaching Profession has long been recognised as affording such opportunities for a pastoral and evangelistic ministry, that schoolmasters and university tutors are accepted for ordination to the priesthood. In this connection it is pertinent to refer to the statement of the *McNair Report*[53] that five or six thousand youth leaders, and at least fifty thousand more school-teachers, will be required after the war. Here is one of the finest opportunities for evangelism that could possibly be offered the Church, if only it can seize it with both hands.

51 *The Churches Survey their Task* (1937), p. 128.
52 See Recommendations, par. 363.
53 *Teachers and Youth Leaders*, H.M.S.O. (1944), pars. 52, 64, 339.

All down the centuries there have been those who have used their *literary gifts* for ends that are definitely evangelistic.

Doctors and nurses are presented with unexampled openings for witness; more especially as theirs is already a Christ-like ministry.

Christian psychiatrists might well be considered for ordination, as commissioned confessors and spiritual directors of the Church.

In the Services, officers are trained to consider themselves the guide, philosopher and friend of their men.

Lawyers and those who hold colonial appointments are brought into intimate contact every day with those seeking help and counsel.

There is *Welfare Work* of all kinds, and more in view (such as the practice of preventive medicine), much of which used to be part of the pastoral responsibility of the parish priest.

In *industry and commerce* there are an increasing number of posts which give scope for Christian influence from within, and bring those who occupy them into touch with multitudes outside the Church.

Finally, when we remember the hunger for fellowship among people generally, which has occasioned such a remarkable increase of *holiday camps and refreshment and community centres,* and when we recall the success that always seems to attend evangelism at camps and holiday homes and informal gatherings, is there not here a new and fruitful field lying fallow for Gospel sowing?

140   In all that we have said we would emphasise the truth—so **The spirit** evident in the ministry of Him who went about teaching, preach-**of evangelism.** ing and healing[54]—that evangelism is not a specialised activity, nor can its duties be strictly defined. Rather it springs from an attitude of mind and heart which sees all the relationships and activities of this life in the light of God's relationship to man, and of His power to redeem the whole of life through the Gospel of Jesus Christ.

We must now ask, how can the whole Church, mobilized and trained for evangelism, proclaim the Gospel to all our countrymen, and prepare their hearts to receive it?

---

[54] Matt. iv, 23 and ix, 35.

APPENDED NOTE ON PRIESTS IN INDUSTRY

The Commission appointed a sub-committee "to consider how the Church is to make contact with the industrial community, with special reference to the possibility of men exercising their priesthood in industry."

The Committee consisted of Mr. G. Bromby, Captain L. W. Chidzey, C.A., the Rev. R. de Pemberton, the Rev. St. J. B. Groser, Miss Knight-Bruce, Mr. J. B. Peile, Canon S. E. Swann, the Rev. H. Treacher, the Rev. Mervyn Stockwood (Chairman).

The following kindly attended to give evidence:—The Bishop of Coventry, Sir Stafford Cripps (Minister of Aircraft Production), Mr. G. Clutton Brock (Head of Oxford House), Mr. L. Conway (Bristol Electricity Department), the Rev. A. Startin (Industrial Organiser, Coventry), the Rev. E. Stopford (a priest working in industry), Mr. M. Healey (L.M.S. Railway), Mrs. Knapp (an industrial worker), Mr. Alan Jarvis (Welfare Officer and Personnel Manager, Ministry of Aircraft Production), Mr. R. Johnson (Industrial Secretary of the Student Christian Movement).

The Committee was also indebted to an *ad hoc* committee consisting of eight Bristol laymen drawn from industry and agriculture, who met seven times and prepared the material for discussion.

The Committee decided that the question of priests exercising their ministry in industry could not be considered in isolation, but as part of the general strategy of the Church. In facing the problem of evangelisation, the Church must plan how to make the best and most efficient use of its manpower, both clerical and lay. While most clergy will inevitably practise their ministry within the framework of the parochial system, the Committee felt that some may be called to exercise their priesthood in other spheres, of which industry is one. Such a departure from custom has obvious dangers, but this cannot be as serious as those which would result from a refusal to make experiments. The future of the country is being fashioned to a considerable extent in the factories and workshops. It is, therefore, essential that alert and able churchmen should be in key positions to influence and lead industrial thought. In executing such a strategical plan a Christian should not be excluded merely because he is in Holy Orders. On the contrary the authority which attaches to his office, as deacon or priest, should be an advantage. The Committee made three recommendations:—

1. In some circumstances, a parish priest should be allowed to take a job in industry for a shorter or longer period.

The change would benefit the Church in so far as it would give the priest a better understanding of the working population of this country. Moreover, it might break down some of the popular prejudices if the workers were to find themselves standing alongside an ordained representative of the Church who was sharing the difficulties, problems and frustrations of their lives. Although it is unlikely that many clergy will feel themselves called to make the offer, it is arguable that candidates for the ministry should be encouraged to spend some months in a factory, or on the land, before ordination.

The Committee would urge that similar opportunities should be given to Deaconesses and Women Workers.

2. In exceptional circumstances, an industrial worker should be ordained as a deacon or priest, to remain in industry and exercise his ministry as an industrial worker. Similarly, a woman worker might become a Deaconess.

If any large-scale attempt is to be made to Christianise industry, it will be necessary to develop a strategy which will depend upon a network of well organised and carefully trained cells. These cells will normally be led by laymen; but in some instances a number of allied groups may wish to submit to the Bishop the name of one of their members for ordination. It would be the duty of such a priest in industry to act as the authoritative representative of the Church in factory life, and to determine and correlate strategy. He would use his lunch hours for propaganda work and instruction, and he would visit his fellow workers after factory hours. He would take a prominent part in trade union and municipal affairs. In some cases it might be practicable for him to be licensed to a city church and to use it as a centre for instruction and worship.

It was agreed that the educational requirements of such a priest would be different from those of the parish priest, and it should be left to the discretion of the Bishop to decide the nature and length of training.

3. The parish priest should make use of existing opportunities to visit the factories in his parish and to get to know the workers.

The Committee was convinced that much can be accomplished by a sympathetic priest who is ready to devote time to this work. Discussion groups, padre's hours, brains trusts, instruction courses and occasional services have become regular features in some factories; and in most instances they have met with considerable success. Unfortunately, there are still many factories in which a priest is never seen from one end of the year to the other.

It is essential that, in addition to the permission of the management, the goodwill of the workers should be obtained before a priest holds a meeting in a factory.

CHAPTER IV

EVANGELISM. PROCLAIMING THE GOSPEL

"It is quite futile saying to people: 'Go to the Cross.' We must be able to say: 'Come to the Cross.' And there are only two voices which can issue that invitation with effect. One is the voice of the sinless Redeemer, with which we cannot speak; and one is the voice of the forgiven sinner, who knows himself forgiven. That is our part.
WILLIAM TEMPLE.

Preaching the Gospel.

EVANGELISM has been defined as confronting the individual soul with the reality of God in Christ. If such a personal presentation of the Gospel is to win the decisive response of Conversion, two requirements are necessary:—

(1) First, the Gospel must be " proclaimed," as by a herald.[1] In other words, to " preach the Gospel " means preaching Christian dogma.

(2) Secondly, the Gospel must be so presented that a definite decision of the will is demanded. In other words, to " preach the Gospel " involves an appeal to the emotions.

Seeing that both words, *dogma* and *emotion,* are misunderstood and ordinarily suspect, we must set forth in some detail the place of dogma and emotion in evangelism, before outlining their operation in various methods of presenting the Gospel.

THE PLACE OF DOGMA IN EVANGELISM

The meaning of Dogma.

142 Preaching the Gospel and teaching doctrine are sometimes set in opposition to one another. It is true that there can be teaching of doctrine without evangelism, but there can be no true evangelism apart from those fundamental doctrines which are the content of the Good News. Obviously, evangelism—to present Christ to men—is bound to rest upon the great Christian dogmas.

The word *dogma* is unpopular because it has come to imply " an arrogant declaration of opinion."[2] As such, the unpopularity of the word serves a useful purpose, for " dogmatic " preaching can so easily savour of pride. We welcome the warning that, although the presentation of Christ Jesus in the power of the Holy

---

1 I Cor: i, 21. See C. H. Dodd, *The Apostolic Preaching*, p. 1.f.
2 Concise Oxford Dictionary.

Spirit demands preaching with authority, it must yet be with humility and with persuasion. No exception, however, can be taken to the original meaning of dogma, namely, " a settled opinion positively expressed."[3] Indeed, there is good reason for retaining the word in current use, if only as a protest against the popular notion that religious truth (unlike scientific truth) should never be taught with authority.

Christian dogma is revealed truth. It possesses a living and active force, and is also the foundation on which Christian belief and behaviour are based. Out of it emerges Christian doctrine; for doctrine is the formulation of revealed truth in current terms, together with the deductions implicit within it. " Essentially " religious dogmas " are the solutions of the great problems that have never ceased to engage and perplex the mind of man—the nature of reality, the existence of God, the origin of the world, the source of evil, the expiation of sin, the future of humanity. Dogma is the core of every system of faith and worship; without it, religion would dissolve into mere sentiment and would, in a few generations, perish altogether."[4]

143 The great dogmas of Christianity are, thus, the good news of God to men. They constitute a Gospel which cannot be watered down, though their mature apprehension is not at first to be required for " babes in Christ."[5] At the same time, a grasp of doctrine, derived from the Bible as the Word of God, is the essential equipment of an evangelist, and one that has never been more needed than to-day. Whatever may have been the case in the past, the modern evangelist, sowing the seed in the mission field of England, cannot take for granted even that belief in a Higher Power on which the missionary overseas can base his message. The evangelist does, in fact, proclaim dogma in order truly to evangelise; and in all evangelism there is the pre-requisite that those who witness or preach shall be thoroughly grounded in Scriptural doctrine. *Necessary for evangelism.*

144 For this purpose there is a call for more training manuals which set out the message of Christianity, together with the relevant Scripture passages.[6] More particularly, they should elucidate by illustration the ways and means by which the eternal Gospel can be *Training manuals.*

---

3 Nuttall's Dictionary.
4 Prof. E. J. Whittaker, Riddell Memorial Lecture: *The Beginning and the End of the World* (Oxford Univ. Press), p. 5.
5 Cf. Newman· "From the age of fifteen dogma has been the fundamental principle of my religion. I know no other religion. I cannot enter into the idea of any other sort of religion; religion as a mere sentiment is to me a dream and a mockery."
6 See par. 250.

brought home to present day non-worshipping members of the community. Such manuals fail in their purpose unless they themselves are the proof that dogmatic teaching can be the very reverse of dull and heavy.

THE PLACE OF EMOTION IN EVANGELISM

The use of emotion. *145* To accept Christ Jesus as Saviour demands a definite and consciously willed act. To serve Him as King demands the purposed and sustained striving of the will. For this reason St. Paul ascribes a *decisive* significance to faith in Jesus Christ. With him faith " is not merely assent or adhesion but *enthusiastic* adhesion, personal adhesion; the highest and most effective motive power of which human character is capable."[7] Thus (literally translated) a common expression in the New Testament is " to believe *onto* Christ," connoting a drive towards Christ. Accordingly, the emotions are bound to play a leading part in evangelism, for they underlie our springs of action. This explains how the Gospel of Christ works its miracle of salvation and effects its reformation of character. It engenders what Dr. Thomas Chalmers described as " the expulsive power of a new affection."

The danger of emotion-alism. As emotion is, admittedly, so powerful a force in human personality, an appeal to the emotions involves a grave responsibility, demanding both knowledge and restraint in those who make it. Emotion must never be allowed to become an end in itself. Emotionalism, that is emotion separated from an outlet in action, is not strengthening but enfeebling. The ultimate outcome is hysteria. " We do violence to our nature and demoralise ourselves if we do not use emotions as the impetus to conduct, or if we permit ourselves to cultivate them simply for the luxury of having them."[8]

In all evangelism there is the duty of working for a decision of the will. Evangelists, therefore, should take warning that it is incumbent on them to act under the conscious guidance of the Holy Spirit, and in accordance with that respect for personality which was so marked a feature of our Lord's dealing with individuals.

METHODS OF EVANGELISM

Fields for evangelism. *146* The opportunity for evangelism is at least as great to-day as it has ever been in the whole course of Christian history. Behind and beneath contemporary materialism, the war has increasingly disclosed among great numbers, and in very different sections of the

7 Sanday & Headlam: Romans, p. 34.
8 *Encyclopædia of Religion and Ethics*: vol. v, p. 512.

community, an unsatisfied and inarticulate spiritual hunger: a sense
of want rather than the wanting of something.   How is the Church,
in actual practice, to make, once more, its primary business (without
which the rest avails nothing) the offering of the Living Christ as
the full satisfaction of man's need, and to present His claims with
authority and effect to our generation?

It is impossible within the limits of this Report to deal
adequately with the whole range of activities which belongs to the
strategy of evangelism.   We hope that this Report will, in due
course, be supplemented by five pamphlets dealing with Parochial
Missions, General Campaigns, Personal Dealings, Evangelism
among Children, Evangelism and Youth.   In this chapter we can
only attempt to prepare the way by suggesting general lines for
evangelism in towns and villages, to children and young people.

EVANGELISM IN TOWNS

WHETHER in its indirect stage of preparing for the Gospel, **The two**
or in its more direct stage of presenting the Gospel, there are **movements
of evan-**
two movements of evangelism, clearly discernible and easily distin- **gelism.**
guishable.

The one is the expansion of the Church and its Gospel within
society, of which the classic simile is " the leaven in the lump."[9]

The other is the impact of the Church and its Gospel upon
society from without, such as the parable of the *Great Supper*
illustrates, with the servants bidden to " go out into the highways
and hedges and compel them to come in."[10]

Both evangelistic methods are demanded for the presentation
of Christ as Saviour and King in great centres of population.

THE EXPANSION OF CHRISTIANITY WITHIN SOCIETY

148   Even in towns and cities the parish is still, and will largely **Active**
remain, the organic unit of the Church.   The conversion of England **church
fellowship.**
cannot be attempted apart from the parochial system.   Not only
would an evangelistic campaign be abortive which did not work
through the parish churches, but without them there could exist

9 Matt. xiii, 33.
10 Luke xiv, 25.

no fellowship to welcome and build up those who were gathered in.[11]

When, therefore, we speak of evangelising English society by expansion from within, we mean lively parish church fellowships which exert an evangelistic influence upon their neighbourhood, and upon every kind of community within it. This would be effected partly by individual Christians permeating every section of society, and partly by groups of church people planting living centres, or germs, of Christian infection in that particular community in which they spend their working hours.

Group fellowship.
149   If a congregation is to become such a purposeful fellowship, not only is the full co-operation of lay people essential, but they must be mobilised and trained.   There thus arises the need of inner groups within the wider fellowship of the Church. Undoubtedly the creation of inner groups is a policy fraught with difficulty and even with danger. The members of such groups sometimes become eclectic in their attitude to the general congregation, while those without are inclined to be suspicious and resentful of those within.

With all groups, too, there is the distasteful necessity both of keeping out, and of weeding out, unsuitable members. The most satisfactory precaution is the open publication of the rules of fellowship of each particular group, and the exercise of group discipline in their fulfilment. More particularly, as group fellowship cannot be maintained with less than fortnightly meetings, strict insistence on the regular attendance of all members is essential, salutary and sifting.

But whatever the difficulty or danger, these must be faced and risked, for we believe that without such inner groups the work of present day evangelism cannot go forward.

Groups for Evangelism.
150   Based on the principle of small groups, which become more groups and maintain close touch with each other, there are several types of *evangelistic* groups that can operate in a parish. They are not mutually exclusive, and the same person may be a member of two or more of them.

In them all, prayer and waiting upon the Holy Spirit form the fount of their every activity.

Inner groups.
151   *Inner Groups* have been formed with effect within each parochial organization, to evangelise it and to hold it to its spiritual

11 But see Appended Note on Ecumenical Co-operation, p. 96.

purpose. Where such inner groups exist, it is recommended that they all meet as one central and parish group several times a year.

152   Cells for Witness[12] are composed of those who desire by **Cells for witness.** habits of personal devotion, by study, by planning together and by pooling experience, to equip themselves for ordinary everyday witness to Christ in their neighbourhood, at their work, and in whatever parochial activity they may be engaged.[13] They help each other to talk quite naturally about Christ to those among whom they live and move. It is the propaganda method. Miss Mildred Cable calls it "gossiping" about one's faith. She has watched teams of two or three communists spread their doctrines in fifteen years throughout the bazaars of Turkestan, simply by talking about them everywhere.

153   Teams of Witness (or News Teams as they are called by the **Teams of witness.** Church Army)[14] are groups which meet specifically to prepare and train for *public* witness and *organised* evangelistic enterprise. The members seek to equip themselves to take part in house to house visiting, open air and home meetings, missions and campaigns, whether in their own neighbourhood or further afield.

154   Prayer Groups need a special word. Although the normal **Prayer groups.** rule for evangelism, taught and practised by our Lord Himself, is the blending of prayer with work by the agents of evangelism, it is sometimes profitable to call into being (it may be for a period) a band of special "remembrancers"[15] who have a more particular vocation for the ministry of intercession. In this way, too, older and more infirm members of the Church can play a definite part in personal evangelism, by being recruited for this purpose.

155   Vocational Cells are groups of Christians banded together in **Vocational Cells.** a factory or business house to present Christ Jesus to their fellows, and to introduce, or maintain, Christian standards in the conduct of the industry or business in which they are engaged. Very seldom will the members of such groups come from any one parish or even from any one Christian denomination. They are of immense importance in bringing Christ to places where the people are congregated, and His principles to bear upon the life of the nation.[16] The fact,

12 See also pars. 122 and 299.
13 For information about the "Cell" method write to the Hon. Secretary, Advisory Group for Christian Cells, Townsend House, Greycoat Place, London, S.W.1.
14 For information about "News Teams" write to Captain Chidzey, C.A., News Team Secretary, 55 Bryanston Street, London, W.1. See pars 124 and 169.
15 Is. lxii, 6.
16 See pars. 135-137.

therefore, must be recognised and welcomed that denominationalism can play no part in these vocational cells. It is only by means of a united Christian front that we can hope to Christianise industry and commerce.

There is no call either for misgiving or non-co-operation in this vital matter. The Student Christian Movement has, during the present century, been recognised as the strongest force for religion in the universities of the world. The S.C.M. is inter-denominational in character. It could not be otherwise if it is to be effective in student communities with their various church loyalties. The same principle is bound to obtain in all other closely knit bodies, such as those in which most people find their vocation.[17]

THE IMPACT OF CHRISTIANITY UPON SOCIETY

Evangelism in action. *156* In days when there is no general movement of religious revival, evangelism will be chiefly successful by pursuing the method of expansion from within. We have likened this personal method to the working of leaven, and its chief requirements are that the leaven must possess pungency, and also that it must be *in the lump* and not shut up in the Church as in a tin.

At the same time the other method of impact upon society from without must also be employed with vigour, even when sensational results cannot be expected.

All and every means of evangelism should be employed. The suggestion that the Parochial Mission is an outworn expedient is one which Screwtape told Wormwood to put into circulation. But new methods, such as General Campaigns, must also be thought out and tried out, and the experience thus gained pooled for the benefit of the whole Church.

Owing to the complexity of the times, it is impossible to lay down hard and fast rules of evangelistic strategy. We content ourselves by giving an outline of the purposes served by Parochial Missions and General Campaigns, which we hope will be filled out later in pamphlets. We would also encourage adventurous enterprise and experiment by pointing to three guiding principles that emerge from our definition of evangelism—*the presentation of Christ Jesus to men in the power of the Holy Spirit.*

17 See Appended Note on Ecumenical Co-operation, p. 96.

GUIDING PRINCIPLES

157   If it is *Christ Jesus* we are to present to men, then the *whole* Christ must be lifted up if He is to draw all men to Himself.   Failure in evangelism in the past has been partly due to a tendency, in preachers of the Gospel, to present an imperfect picture of our Lord. They have been apt to concentrate on that particular aspect of His Person and Work which made the most appeal to them personally. Every mission or campaign, and every series of addresses, should present Christ in all His fulness.   Very shortly, this involves a threefold presentation.   *1. Presenting the whole Christ.*

There is the Christ of the Bible to be preached, as set forth in the Creeds. This involves driving home the events of the Gospel story (together with their meaning) as historical realities.

There is the Christ of history to be proclaimed, His victories down the centuries to be made known, and how His Body, the Church, has moulded civilization, spread throughout the world and initiated all movements of social betterment and reform.

There is the Christ of personal experience to be declared, and the fact of his ever-abiding Presence, bestowing the peace of forgiveness, giving power to live victoriously and assuring of eternal life.

158   If it is *to men* that Christ Jesus is to be presented, then we must go to the people, and not expect them to come to us.   Christ must be lifted up in the factory and at the street corner, not only in churches where non-worshippers are unlikely to be found.   *2. Going to the people.*

Some words of the late Archbishop William Temple to the Upper House of Convocation are apposite here: " One sympathetic but detached person said to me : ' When the clergymen comes and takes a service in a canteen or in a cinema, it seems more real and genuine; what goes on in church seems artificial.'   I believe that this is a widespread feeling. If so, we must take it into consideration."[18]

The value of open air services is, largely, that they demonstrate unmistakably that the local church believes it has a truth of vital importance to deliver, and is not afraid or ashamed to proclaim it. Within recent years, Religion and Life, and Industrial Christian Fellowship, campaigns have been successful in reaching those outside our churches in proportion as their meetings were held in the places where the people worked and congregated.

18 *Chronicle of Convocation*, 1942, No. 3 (October), p. 317.

3. Uniting for evangelism. *159* If it is *in the power of the Holy Spirit* that Christ Jesus is to be presented, then we must demonstrate to the world the reality of *the fellowship of the Holy Ghost*. As is well known, the divisions of Christendom prevent very many of those outside the churches from listening seriously to the message of Christianity."[19]

On the other hand, we repeat our conviction that behind every evangelistic effort there must be the existing fellowship of some local church into which converts can immediately be welcomed, and then built up in the Faith.[20] Not sufficient thought has yet been given to the problem of impressing non-worshipping members of the community with the spectacle of the churches united in action, and at the same time of offering to the outsider the immediate fellowship of some one particular church.

United, but parallel, campaigns seem to afford the best solution in present circumstances. A parallel campaign does not mean identity of effort, with all the meetings arranged in one central building, and all ministers of religion speaking from the same platform. In a parallel campaign, certain joint meetings and services are arranged in order to express to those outside that bond of unity in the Holy Spirit which animates those taking part. For example, a united procession to the commissioning service, and a united act of thanksgiving to conclude the campaign, would strike the required and arresting note.

In the main, however, in a parallel campaign, each church organises and conducts its own mission; but at the same time, and on the same lines, as the rest. In this way, while presenting a united front, each church is able to draw into its own body those who have been brought into touch with its fellowship. Experience would seem to show that co-operation with the Free Churches on such parallel lines should, where circumstances permit, be attempted, if not in the case of Parochial Missions, at any rate with General Campaigns.[21] About both of these we must now speak shortly.

PAROCHIAL MISSIONS

The first essential. *160*   **It is disastrous, and worse than useless, to attempt a Parochial Mission of any kind unless, not only has the preparation been ample, but the "follow up" has been carefully planned and**

---

19 See par. 75.
20 See par. 148, and also 168.
21 See also Appended Note on Ecumenical Co-operation, p. 96.

the promoters have satisfactorily answered the question, "What do you propose to do with those whose hearts are touched?"

THE TEACHING CONVENTION

161   A Teaching Convention is a coming together of the people of a parish to receive consecutive instruction in the essential truths and practices of the Christian religion.   Its *aim* is to teach and explain the substance of Christian faith and life.   It attempts to present the Christian religion as a *whole,* linking conduct with belief, witness with worship, service with sacrament.   It seeks to enlighten the mind, to direct the will and to incline the heart towards a deeper fellowship with God.   It is an attempt to reinforce and to encourage the parish priest in the fulfilment of his commission "to teach, and to premonish, to feed and provide for the Lord's family." *The aim of a Teaching Convention.*

Systematic teaching should be the normal function of every parochial ministry.   It is, however, unfortunately true that many church people are lamentably ignorant of the Christian Faith, either because systematic teaching is not given, or because they themselves attend church so irregularly that they never learn to see the principles and practices of their religion *as a whole*.   The Church to-day lacks converting power because the majority of its members are not convinced Christians.   The widespread ignorance of the most elementary truths of the Christian religion makes it imperative that the laity should understand their faith and commend it in word and deed.

But while the *appeal* of the Parochial Convention is primarily to Church-people—regular, indifferent, lapsed and nominal; many who are dissatisfied with their own religion (whatever it is), and many who are seeking a religion, welcome the opportunity of hearing the case for Christianity as it is dealt with in the Convention. The Convention thus makes a great appeal to those outside the Church as well as to those within.

It is an essential part of the preparation for a Convention that every house in the parish should be visited twice, and that the visitor should make personal contact with the household.

162   A Teaching Convention normally lasts one week, services being held every night at a time suitable to the people of the parish.   The subject-matter of the teaching is generally the Christian faith and life.   The method and technique of the Con- *The conduct of a Teaching Mission.*

vention can, also, be used profitably in dealing with one or more aspects of Christian truth and practice, as, for example, prayer and worship, the work of the Church overseas, the application of Christian principles to social and economic problems.

It is important to remember always that, whatever the nature of the teaching given, the parish priest must prepare for it in his preaching and continue with it afterwards. The Convention must be prepared for and followed up both in the pulpit and in the parish.

Schools for Conductors. *163*   Experience has proved the great value of the Parochial Convention, and there is a growing demand for an effort of this kind by parishes of all types. But there are not the conductors available. It is not simple required of a conductor that he should know what to teach. He must know how to teach what he knows, and he must be able to teach from the heart as well as from the mind. The Convention has a special method and technique, which must be learnt. The need is training. Schools for Conductors should be held. Certain dioceses have experience of these and know their great value. Much more in the way of training needs to be done for work of this kind.

THE EVANGELISTIC MISSION

The evangelistic aim. *164*   A Parochial Mission is an evangelistic effort on a grand scale that arouses attention. It is an attempt to preach the Gospel to everyone who can be reached in a particular parish or area. Its primary aim is conversion. It summons men to repentance and newness of life. It calls those who have as yet made no decision for Christ to do so. It also aims at helping those who are already within the Church to gain a deeper sense of responsibility for those outside.

The Missioner. *165*   The demands made upon a missioner are great. He must be a man lost in his message. He must believe that the message has the power to change men's lives. He must be filled with hope for those who are seemingly hopeless. He must have infinite patience in dealing with individuals. He must understand their sins and difficulties. He must know what remedies the Gospel proposes and how the assurance of forgiveness may be found. His message must be much more than an emotional appeal. The Holy Spirit, speaking through him, will make men ask: "What shall we do?'' He must know the answer. He must also be able to build men up in the faith and fellowship of the Church; for a Parochial Mission which ignores the intellect and relies on emotion, is not likely to have lasting results.

THE PREPARATION FOR PAROCHIAL MISSIONS.

166   Much of the success of a Convention or Mission will depend **Prepara-** on the preparation beforehand. The whole congregation must be **tion.** mobilised, and from them a band of workers must be trained. As far as possible every house in the parish must be visited, and the workers who undertake this task must be prepared to witness by word of mouth, if need be. They should also be willing to take part in such outdoor ventures as may be planned to awaken the parish to the approaching mission. All this will need careful training by the parish priest, especially in prayer and in the ways of effective witness. Before, during, and after the mission the workers will have their part to play; for they should not only pave the way but also help to consolidate the gains.

Nor should the preparation be confined to those enrolled as workers. Side by side with their preparation should go the preparation of the whole congregation. Everyone should be encouraged to join in the prayer groups and special intercession services. All should take part in the outdoor services and processions, if these are held. All should feel that they are personally involved in the venture.

It is vital that an intensification of the spirit of fellowship should be an objective of the preparation. It would be of little use to hold a mission unless those who are converted by it and, perhaps, brought to church for the first time, find within the Body of Christ a warmth of welcome which breaks down the natural barriers between man and man. In part this intensification of fellowship will develop from the sense of responsibility in the common task. In part it can be secured by the fostering of the mission spirit in those organisations through which the social life of the parish normally functions.

SOME RECENT EXPERIMENTS

167   Normally a missioner pays a visit or visits to the parish to **1. Meeting** preach and to meet the workers. In the past these visits have **the Mis-** usually occurred a considerable time before the mission itself **sioner.** and the missioner has confined his contacts to the congregation.

Some parishes, however, have felt the need for a closer contact
between the missioner and those for whom the mission is intended.
As part, therefore, of the preparation, a "Meet the Missioner Week"
has been held as a prelude to the mission itself.

Recently an experiment on these lines was made in a small
north-country town. The two missioners came to the town on the
Monday of the week before the mission was due to begin. Every
house in the parish received an invitation to gatherings where the
missioners could be met. There was a social evening. On
other days there were various "Neighbour Meetings" in private
houses in different parts of the parish. Some of these were tea-
parties to which the guests brought their own food. The result was
a mixture of all social ranks. Some of the tea-parties were held in
the larger houses, and some in cottages. To all these social gatherings one or other of the missioners came. They spoke about their
work in previous missions, established friendly contacts and ended
with an appeal for regular attendance at the mission.

Difficulties thus overcome. *168*   By this venture certain obstacles were overcome. One of
the main difficulties is to establish contact between individuals and
the missioner. It is almost inevitable that, where there has been no
friendly contact, the missioner must appear as a remote and rather
austere figure. The result is that many hesitate to get into touch
with him.

Another difficulty is that some only wake up to the fact that
the mission is being held when it is already well on its way. The
missioner must either begin all over again, or the late-comers miss
some of the most vital teaching.

A "Meet the Missioner Week" helps to overcome both these
difficulties. It forces the mission on the notice of people. Because
of the personal contacts already made, the people are less shy of
approaching him during the mission. In the case of the mission
mentioned, intimate conversation began on the morning of the
second day, and continued throughout the week.

2. The use of lay witnesses. *169*   In recent years successful use has been made of lay witnesses
to support the missioner in his appeal. The value of such witness is
that it is " lay." The " professional " evangelist is often suspect
because he is " paid to do the job." It is, therefore, of great value
if the missioner can demonstrate the truth and power of the Gospel
by the introduction of lay witnesses who can speak from personal
experience of the truths with which the missioner is dealing. What
these witnesses say should be said shortly and simply and have a

direct bearing on the theme of the missioner's address. They work with the missioner as a team. Church Army "News Teams"[22] have been of considerable use in this direction. Witness should not be in the form of " sermonettes," but a simple affirmation of faith based on personal experience. The witnesses are also encouraged to work in a personal way amongst those who attend the mission. Such witnessing needs humility and much prayerful preparation. It is advisable that the team of witnesses should come from outside the parish.

170   Many parishes, especially those with large populations, are **3. Workers** daunted at the prospect of a mission because the ground to be **from other** covered seems to be beyond the capacity of the congregation. In **parishes.** such cases help may well be sought from other parishes, and there are instances where this has been done with benefit both to the helping and the helped parish. Co-operation has led to the helping parish feeling the need of a mission for itself. Workers from other parishes should be prepared to undergo a training similar to that of those from within the parish.

THE FUTURE OF PAROCHIAL MISSIONS

171   Doubts are sometimes expressed as to the usefulness of **Their** Parochial Missions to-day. It has been pointed out that they no **value.** longer attract the outsider as they used to do. This is certainly true; not only because of the increasing number of counter-attractions, but also because the scepticism of to-day makes people unwilling to be "caught" and committed to beliefs which will involve definite decisions.

We are, however, convinced that the day of Parochial Missions is by no means over. The very fact that a parish is prepared to make great efforts to reach the outsider is in itself a valuable witness to the conviction that the Church has a Gospel to proclaim. Even if the outsiders who attend are few in number, the effort to reach them has a most bracing effect upon the congregation. Those who have worked and prayed for the mission will, at least, have learnt to understand their evangelistic responsibilities as members of the Body of Christ. The value of a parochial mission can never be assessed in numbers, nor can its true results be estimated at the time. The real results may only appear many years afterwards.

The whole important question of the "follow-up" of Parochial Missions will be dealt with in the pamphlet now in preparation.

22 See pars. 124 and 153.

GENERAL CAMPAIGNS

Evangelistic *172*   A Parochial Mission is confined to one parish. An
Campaigns. Evangelistic Campaign is wider in scope and tackles a neighbourhood. Such Campaigns are of four kinds.

1. Area *173*   A group of churches in an area may combine in a common
Campaigns. evangelistic effort to reach the unconverted. Such a campaign may
be described as a Parochial Mission on a large scale. It is either
carried on, simultaneously, in a number of different centres; or else
parishes combine to hold their meetings in one centre. Because it
is on a large scale it arouses the attention and excites the interest
of non-worshipping members of the community.

The plan has been tried, with success, of the clergy and laity
of a group of parishes in a Deanery, combining together to run a
campaign in one parish. Such action develops a new spirit of
fellowship between the parishes. It brings effective help to the
parish in which the campaign is held. Above all it provides an
opportunity for the clergy and laity to learn how to evangelise.[23]

2. Sectional *174*   Campaigns designed to reach a particular constituency are
Campaigns. of old standing, and have proved their evangelistic value. To this
category belong such special efforts as Industrial Christian Fellow-
ship, Crusades, Student and Youth Campaigns, Hop-Pickers'
Missions, Church Army Van Missions, Harvest and Holiday
Camps. There is sometimes discernible in some of them a tendency
not to press for definite acceptance of Christ Jesus as Saviour and
King. The day for this hesitation has passed, if it ever dawned.

3. Prepara- *175*   Sometimes a Campaign is designed to prepare the way for a
tory
Campaigns. Parochial Mission. Before the seed of the Gospel can be sown there
is the need to break up the fallow ground, to remove prejudice
and ignorance, to root out wrong ideas; in a word, to prepare men's
minds to receive the Gospel. Such a Campaign is often a joint
effort by a number of parishes; each of which follows it up with a
Parochial Mission. Unless this is the intention, particular pains
must be devoted to the "follow-up," such as will be outlined in
the forthcoming pamphlet.

4. Long- *176*   Another type of Campaign altogether is that which does not
term Cam-
paigns. consist in a series of public meetings, but in the formation of a
number of groups of Christian men and women who, over a period

23 See par. 103.

of months or years, will seek to influence the locality where they live, or the place in which they work. There are many who feel that this type of Campaign holds out the highest hopes for the future; more particularly as the age of big public meetings seems to have passed, at any rate for a time.

VILLAGE EVANGELISM

SO far what we have said in this Report, though largely applicable to evangelism in any sphere, has had the town situation chiefly in mind. This in no way indicates any lack of appreciation of the importance of village evangelism. Indeed, many believe that the hope of the future lies in the country; and that in the event of a national revival of religion it will be in the countryside that the seed will have been sown, from whence it will spread to our towns and cities. *A complex situation.*

The chief difficulty in speaking of village evangelism lies in the fact that hardly two villages are circumstanced alike. They vary from the outlying suburb of a neighbouring town to the utter isolation of an inter-married clan, and from the busy centre of a local industry to scattered hamlets miles away even from their parish church.

Furthermore, modern village life has not found itself. The development of road transport is rapidly urbanizing rural areas, and revolutionizing the traditional outlook and behaviour of the countryside. In such a fluid state of change few experiments in specifically village evangelism have as yet been possible, and it is still too soon to judge the effect of those which have been attempted. Several important committees are giving much thought to the whole question of village Christianity and community life; but their conclusions are necessarily hypothetical and await the test of practical experience.[24]

178 Very much that we have suggested regarding evangelism in general is thoroughly pertinent to villages and only requires to be specially applied to meet the circumstances of each particular parish. Thus, the section dealing with evangelism through groups or cells is extremely relevant. Prayer groups, discussion groups, study circles and teams for witness have already been tried out in country parishes with conspicuous success. *The country parson.*

24 E.g. The Rural Reconstruction Group of the British Council of Churches. The Church's Group for the Countryside. The Council for the Church and the Countryside.

Also, all that has been said about the parish priest being the key to the evangelistic situation has even greater force when applied to the country clergy. It was rural England that adopted for its use the name of " Parson," the *persona,* or personage, of the parish. He is the expected leader of every sort of activity; and that where the dearth of leadership is often an acute problem. Without his goodwill, evangelism through groups or cells is hardly possible in most villages.

In a country parish, too, the Occasional Offices afford pre-eminent opportunities for evangelism. Indeed, pastoral work at its best may be said to be the best evangelistic method. Owing to the traditional and steady routine of country life, George Herbert's *The Country Parson* still holds good as one of the best expositions of what a village ministry demands. Are the parson and his wife loving and amicable people, and such as the villagers can grow to love, respect and trust? If so, the first great step towards a "converted" village has been achieved.

Again, the emphasis we have laid on the importance of translating technical theological expressions into terms understood by ordinary people, is particularly needed when the congregation is a country one. In a rural community there is demanded of the parson, for preaching and teaching, not less learning but in addition a high order of intellectual discipline and a long apprenticeship in the use of words, if the truths of the Gospel are to be conveyed in intelligible language.

Difficulty yet hope. *179*   Our special task must be to explain the peculiar difficulties that confront evangelism in the modern country parish, and then to point to the particular opportunities presented by the changing times.

In so doing, we would enlist the understanding prayer of the whole Church on behalf of that great body of country clergy who, beset with the temptations that accompany isolation, yet bear the sole responsibility of the spiritual life of whole communities, and are often faced with baffling perplexities in a complex situation.

We would, at the same time, echo the note of hope for village evangelism which has reached us from many quarters. The stability of the country-side, coupled with the awakening processes now entering into it, give promise of a good response to experiment and leadership; if only the village is regarded as an active and adventurous sphere for a pioneer, and not as a suitable place of retirement for a tired man.

Obstacles to Village Evangelism

180   *Lack of Unity* is the chief obstacle to evangelism. It is the **1. Lack of unity.** natural outcome of the transitional stage through which the village is passing. The opening up of the countryside by road transport is bringing to bear upon it strong urban influences.   There is no disputing the immense material amenities and advantages which have accrued thereby.   But we are here concerned with the change effected upon outlook and behaviour. These present, at the moment, those "adolescent" characteristics which are to be expected in the passage from one stage of development into another.   Modern village life often seems to combine the less satisfactory features of town and country, and has not yet found itself.   The traditional virtues of the old order are fast disappearing, but await replacement by the benefits of the new.

181   The one long standing institution that remains is the village **The village church.** church, dominating the village street, and with its immemorial story as old as English history.   But Mother Church (like the parent of a growing child) has not only to adjust herself to the new circumstances, but is also likely to encounter that suspicion and aggressiveness which usually accompany the acquiring of self-consciousness.

Thus, country folk still retain their innate conservatism and are generally resentful of change.   Many a village church has been emptied by innovations introduced by a new incumbent who is not consonant with the slow and stable rhythm of country life.

At the same time, the newly gained social and economic independence of the farm labourer is apt to express itself by an abstention from Sunday worship.   It is an unconscious protest against the old days when the master expected his men and their families to attend church.

Charabancs and private cars, too, race through the countryside each Lord's Day, heralding the "glad tidings" that urban enlightenment has exploded the ancient "fetish" of Sunday observance and worship.

182   *Lack of leadership* is the other inevitable consequence of the **2. Lack of Leadership.** break-up of the family pattern of village life, occasioned by the development of transport by road and rail. The squire is disappearing, and his place is far too often taken by the non-churchgoing week-ender.   The doctor and the teacher motor in from the neighbouring town.   An increasing number of children are conveyed each day to central schools, and grow up out of touch with the place where their nights are spent.

On the other hand, where the old leaders remain, their leadership has become less acceptable. Or if newcomers to the country show interest in the community around them, they are often regarded with suspicion. The result is a dearth of lay-leadership which constitutes a major problem for the country parson.

The village hall. *183* Meanwhile, democratic organizations, such as the Women's Institute and the committee of the village hall, are beginning to assume leadership; and tend, with their newly-acquired responsibility, to be suspicious and resentful of clerical authority or interference.

Such democratic institutions offer a grand scope for quiet leadership by the parish priest and his wife, if only they look for no preferential treatment, but are glad to be one among many. In particular we would draw attention to the unique opportunity for influence presented by the Young Farmers' Club movement, which many country parsons have been able to turn to magnificent account. Too often the clergy are inclined to look askance at community enterprises which do not centre on the church; instead of seeing in them a sphere of usefulness for the church to serve.

OPPORTUNITIES FOR VILLAGE EVANGELISM

The opportunities. *184* The special opportunities for evangelism which a village affords are threefold in character. There is the opportunity afforded by the common interest in the land; there is the opportunity afforded in the building up of community life; there is the opportunity afforded through close personal relationships.

1. The land. *185* *A common interest in the land* dominates country life. Nearness to nature affects the outlook of all (even of those villagers not directly concerned with agriculture) and forms the basis of their community life together. If, therefore, the parson is himself country-minded, he not only enters into a natural fellowship, but a fellowship that is naturally religiously inclined.

The land offers a creative activity that is sacramental of God's Providence. Those who work on the land live too near Nature, and are too dependent on the swing of the seasons, to forget God in their calling. The country clergy are not, therefore, faced with that materialistic outlook which their brethren in the towns have to break down before their people can see God. Instead, the soil of a village ministry is fallow ground for Gospel sowing. For his services and sermons the village parson has the same material as our Lord Himself found adequate to illustrate and drive home the truths of the Kingdom.

186 For this reason Harvest Festival services have for long ranked with the chief Christian feasts in rural estimation. And now, the revival of the ancient observance of Plough-Sunday, Rogation-tide, and Lammas Day, are meeting with a cordial response. Old customs appeal especially to country people who like to do what their great-grandfathers did. By such observances the workers on the land feel that their labours for their fellowmen are hallowed and blessed by God. Thereby the Church enters into every period of the farm year, and the farmer becomes bound to the Church. Thereby also the rhythm of agricultural life begins to beat out the theme—" Recognise God as the Source and Origin of all life, and then learn to recognise Him in everyday life."

Country festivals.

It is, of course, true that all this concerns natural, rather than revealed, religion. There still remains the requirement of proclaiming Christ's Gospel of redemption from sin—often a difficult matter with stolid sons of the soil. But an awareness of God and of the unseen can be taken for granted when preaching or teaching the Christian faith, and relied on to the full.

187 It must always be remembered that country people view their parson and their church through country eyes. To rid the country clergy of the monstrous burden of acres of garden is a matter of spiritual, as well as of practical, necessity. A parson's garden run to seed is a stumbling block to his flock. Similarly, whether or no church services are worth while is largely judged by whether the churchyard is well cared for or a wilderness. "If the critical eyes of country worshippers are met with a churchyard which suggests neglect, slackness and dishonour to the dead, it will be harder for them to worship than if they are welcomed by a garden of order and beauty."[25]

The vicarage garden.

188 *The building up of village community life* (under the new conditions we have described) calls for the leadership of the country clergy, and thus affords them scope for evangelism. A return to the past, when almost every village happening was centred in the parson and the parish church, is neither possible nor desirable. But by identifying himself and his work with all the varied activities

2. Community life.

25 *The Church in Country Parishes*, p. 33. (The Bishop of Winchester's Report, 1940. S.P.C.K.)

of village life, instead of confining himself to fostering fellowship among his congregation alone, the country parson can bring the power of religion to bear upon the whole neighbourhood.

The clergy still occupy a position in most country parishes which enables them to exercise a considerable influence. They can use their traditional prestige to bring all sections together to work for the whole. They can organise centres and clubs on a community rather than on a church basis. Through their leadership the Church can take the initiative in espousing rural needs and improvements. By so doing, they will bring home to all and sundry the vital truth that Christianity is not just a " side-show," but has an essential contribution to make to all the dominant interests of daily life. The result will be a parish, together with its every activity, that is a field for evangelism.

3. Personal relation-ships. *189   Personal Relationships* particularly characterise a village ministry. The individual approach will thus often afford the best opportunity for presenting Christ Jesus as Saviour and King to those into whose common calling and life God has already entered through the ministry of the church and the leadership of its minister.

Seeing that it may be said of countrymen that "a stranger will they not follow," evangelism in the country depends on knowing and being known. Does the country parson share in the whole life of the village? Is he the father of his people? If so, his evangelistic opportunity may come at any moment, and with any member of his flock. He must, therefore, be always on the alert, always in the Spirit to meet the shy advance, and always ready to turn from trivialities to the deepest realities.

Only a daily time of communion with God, and a continual walk with God, can qualify him to fulfil the conditions of village evangelism. It is essentially a one-by-one garnering of hand-picked fruit. "The fisher of men in a modern [country] parish is not one who casts his net into the sea and gathers in of every kind. He is more like a dry-fly man on an over-fished river; the fish are sophisticated, and he must watch for a ' rise '; sermons may be tried like flies; they may or may not attract, but the striking and landing are done by interviews."[26]

Evangelistic impact from with-out. *190   This emphasis on the evangelistic method of individual approach must not be interpreted as ruling out the method of impact from without. On the contrary, the individual approach is the essential preparation, if the employment of other and

[26] A. W. Hopkinson: *Pastor's Progress,* p. 110.

special methods from outside are to prove effective. Country ministries are generally long and intimate ministries, with the feel of a family relationship about them. In such relationships, a new voice and a fresh approach will often supply the needed spark to set aflame a carefully laid fire. It is unusual, for example, for parents to be used of God to effect the last decisive stage in the conversion of their children, though no conversion would have been likely without their fostering.

Among other agencies, Church Army Van Missions are well-known for their successful village evangelism. If, therefore, the development of transport is largely responsible for the break up of the old order of village life, and for depriving it of lay-leadership, the Church can also turn it to good effect by bringing outside influences to bear upon the no longer isolated village community. Teams of witness from neighbouring towns can be brought in to visit country parishes. Bands of teachers and leaders from outside, under trained organisers, can infuse new life and hope into village Sunday Schools and youth organisations. Above all, the experiment has yet to be tried of alliances between town and country parishes.

191   But when all has been said or done, it still remains true that the parish priest will often be almost the sole agent of evangelism in many an isolated village. The demand thus made upon his spiritual life is immense. But he has the compensation—denied to his brethren in town parishes—of having personal knowledge of every individual in his cure of souls. This presents him with the possibility of exercising a ministry of intercession which has proved, in known instances, to be quite startling in its results. Such a ministry of intercession, to be effective, must be a first call upon his activities, and his visiting largely becomes the gathering of material for his prayers. *An intercessory ministry.*

EVANGELISM AMONG CHILDREN.

IT is impossible to exaggerate the importance of bringing children to a simple and definite trust in God, by their acceptance of Christ Jesus as their Saviour and Friend. *Its Importance.*

The Gospel record is clear that it is God's will that children should come to a personal knowledge of Christ in their early years. Indeed, in striking contrast to the other religions of the world, and their non-recognition of childhood's capacity for religion, Jesus was unique in the high value he placed on children's powers of spiritual apprehension, and in the eager advances He made towards them.

Certainly, childhood affords the best opportunity for the implanting of spiritual truth, when the mind is most receptive to lasting impressions, and before it is invaded by the influences of secular environment.

Moreover, it is not sufficiently recognised that neither Christian home influence, nor Christian education, can guarantee that children, as they grow to maturity, will normally attain to a personal knowledge of their Saviour. The experience of the past century and a half of missions overseas has revealed the "problem of the second generation"—the children of original converts from heathendom. It has shown "that every generation of Christians in the Church needs to be converted."(27)

Its aim. *193*   The aim of evangelism among children must be that they shall become *alive* to Christ.(28) Even young children can be led to realise that God counts in everything, through the atmosphere of home and school, and through graded Christian worship. Moreover, teaching of such importance evokes a ready response from them. In general they have to be told that they must wait and prepare themselves before they can fulfil life's big responsibilities. But Jesus needs them now, and they need Him; and they can be as real and true Christians as grown-up people. With this aim in view two approaches can be particularised, though generally they are concurrent and inter-related.

The one approach is to make, periodically, an appeal to *decide for Christ*. It is a call, repeated from time to time, to open the door to the knocking of Someone without.

The other approach is the constant appeal *to make decisions for Christ*. It is a continual call to act in obedience to Someone already within.

The two approaches correspond to "sudden" and "gradual" conversion and, whether employed separately or together, both of them have been manifestly owned of God.

In the case of a definite call to decide for Christ, undue pressure and unwise emotion must be scrupulously avoided; but it should come to every child before the change from Primary to Secondary education. It can be given through Sunday School

27 Dr. W. W. Cash: *The Missionary Church*, p. 204.
28 See par. 73.

lessons on Great Christians who made a definite decision for Christ (St. Matthew, St. Augustine of Hippo, John Newton), or by a Children's Mission, or at a Children's Service which leads up to a hymn of decision—such as "O Jesus I have promised." In many cases there will be immediate results. In other cases a lasting impression is often made, so that a sudden conversion in later years can be traced to a remembered appeal in childhood.

EVANGELISING AGENCIES

194   Because of their immaturity, it is usual to seek to lead **Gradual** children forward on a course of gradual conversion, when the **Conversion.** Christian life becomes a constant succession of acts of surrender to Christ and of seeking to please Him.   For such growth " in the grace and knowledge of our Lord and Saviour," there are three contributing factors: home training in the Christian faith and life, the progressive teaching and influence of Day and Sunday Schools, and the worship of the Church.   As we now deal with each of them, it must be remembered that none of them will prove effective if their object is merely to sow seed and not also to reap a harvest. Wisely, but decisively, there must be kept constantly before children the claim of Jesus Christ for their trust and loyalty.

195   *Christian Home Life* is the natural and normal introduction **1. The** of the child to the family of God; and Christianity derives its chief **Christian** symbolism and its chief virtues from the life of the family.   A child's **Home.** earliest experience of family affection, and of the laws of family unity, is the purposed and ordained "sacrament" both of the love of God and also of the fellowship of the Church.   Furthermore, the home is intended to provide him with ideals for interpreting and judging all subsequent social experience, and for completing and unifying his social ideas in the notion of a universal Divine family.

For this reason, in evangelism among children, every effort must be made to convert the home as well as the child.   Every child in touch with the Church must be regarded not as an isolated unit, but as opening the door for the winning of the whole family.

196   *Christian Teaching* centres on the Person and work of the **2. Christian** Son of God—at once the Jesus of the Gospel story, the Christ of the **teaching,** Church all down the ages and throughout the world, and the Saviour **centred on** of personal experience.   Only so can He become a living and ever- **Christ.** present reality to children: a fact which demands that He must first be a living and ever-present reality to their teacher.   Only so, also, can theological dogmas become clear to the mind of a child who thinks in pictures; though in the setting of the Living Christ all the doctrines of the Catholic faith can be taught and understood. Christ thus becomes the "Friend for little children"; a truth not to be conveyed with sentimentality or softness, but with the bracing suggestion that He is a Leader to follow and a Master to obey.

God the Father. *197*   So presented, Christ Jesus is the Way that leadeth to the Father. The Father of our Lord Jesus Christ is shown to be Our Father, and the God of Love becomes real to children. At the same time, in these days there is particular reason that teaching on the love of God should include insistence on the holiness of God and upon His justice, and instruction on the working of His moral laws. Christian teaching, even to children, is incomplete which leaves out altogether the fact of judgment, but gives the idea that "everyone goes to heaven when he dies."

The Holy Spirit. *198*   During their earlier years children have to learn how to discriminate between the world of experience and the world of imagination. They have a natural sense of affinity with unseen realities which may become part of their real experience, before "shades of the prison house begin to close upon the growing boy."

Thus, children can apprehend more readily than is generally realised the conception of God the Holy Spirit, the gift of the ascended Christ, at work in the Church and in the heart of the individual. They can be taught to look forward eagerly to receiving God's gift at Confirmation, as they then make the big decision to surrender their lives to His service.

The Church. *199*   Loyalty to Jesus as one's Leader, and the inclusion of God in one's family life, will readily enable children to realise themselves as members of the fellowship of the Church. Their innate desire to belong to a community makes it easy to develop in them their sense of membership in the Body of Christ, and gives added importance to their inclusion in a Sunday School and their attendance at Church worship.

3. Church worship. *200*   *Children's Services* can themselves be made vehicles of evangelism. Even as the Gospel itself is a combination of mystery and simplicity—both so attractive to children—so a child's worship should combine awe with clarity. By careful planning and the wise choice of hymns, of prayers and acts of devotion, dullness can be avoided and the essential happiness of the Christian life can be instilled in children. In the same way the utterly reverent conduct of the service and demeanour of the conductor, will bring to young worshippers the sense of a Holy God; while the pains devoted to orderly arrangement and behaviour will help to reflect the nature of a Creator Father of law and order. It should be possible, too, by their regular attendance, for children to learn something of the essential elements of Christian worship—praise, thanksgiving, penitence and prayer. And it should be remembered that they are not too young to be taught the practice of silent prayer, of a very simple kind.

PERSONAL EVANGELISM

201   There is no more personal (and, therefore, exacting) ministry **The Worker.** than evangelism among children. With children, persons count for everything. With children, too, evangelism is more especially a matter of personal fostering and of hand-picked fruit. Workers among children are marked people, and Christianity is judged by what sharp little eyes see in them. Children are quick to mark any little inconsistencies, which outweigh with them a general high standard of example—they take that for granted in their elders. Workers among children can never be off their guard. They are dealing with highly impressionable material. The child's mind is like the sensitive film in a camera. At any moment (no one can say when) the shutter may flick and an impression will be recorded which will be developed in later life. Evangelism among children, therefore, demands entire consecration, great watchfulness and constant prayer.

202   Unless the worker knows the environment of each child, and **Personal dealings.** can gain the confidence of the child, little evangelism is possible. Children will not open up or be frank and natural with an elder whom they do not look upon and trust as an understanding friend. At the same time, children possess sensitive consciences; they are aware of their sins, and they often have their own deep needs. It is, therefore, an intense relief and happiness to them when they feel encouraged to confide about their fears and difficulties to some-one in whom they have learned to trust. Often such confidences will be no more than hints which need to be understood and interpreted. This bond of friendship between an elder and a child is itself the best explanation to children of the personal help that is offered to them through the Christian religion. The idea of God's grace is best presented as coming through the Divine Friendship of our Saviour,

Who understands us and enables us to overcome our fears and faults.

Three groups of children.

203   For purposes of evangelism, children may be roughly divided into three groups: those who come from Christian homes and count themselves members of their church; those whose home influence is irreligious and are outside the fellowship of the Church and its ministrations; and those who fall somewhere between these two categories.

It is not generally understood that Children's Missions are designed for those who are already within the Church. They are not a recruiting campaign, and are ineffective if used simply to sow seed. Experience has shown that they are fruitful in proportion as they are employed to reap a harvest; and no harvest can be reaped unless the seed has been first sown.

Those children, therefore, outside the Church must be evangelised by attracting them to join the parochial organisations provided for them. Often this is best accomplished by the children themselves who are already attached to them. They make splendid recruiting agents, and hardly require encouragement to take on the responsibility.

As for the betwixt and betweens, the utmost patience is demanded to encourage in them (often against the influence of the home) regular habits of attendance at Church worship, Sunday School or week-day organisations. A holiday campaign, in which games and excursions are included, will prove more effective than a Mission in reaching them and making friends with them. It is better still, if possible, to get them by themselves at a camp or a house party, and away from the deadening influence of their homes or neighbourhood.

EVANGELISM AND YOUTH.

Youth a key position in Evangelism.

THE claiming of each generation of youth for the service of Christ and His Church, is at the very heart of the whole strategy of evangelism.

The period of adolescence is essentially an age of decision, when youth with its idealism and enthusiasm responds to the big claim—the bigger the better.

Also, with its new-found sense of responsibility and adventure, youth is eager to enlist for service; nor is it daunted by the hard task.

Not only do young people themselves make some of the best evangelists of youth, but also the whole Church becomes anæmic without the continual recruitment of their vision and vigour.

205   Youth is the age for decision, one way or the other: " there **An age of** are no half-way houses, no compromises, in a young man's creed. **decision.** It's swallow all or be damned to you.   It's believe or be lost."[29]

It is the time of self-realisation when, with the attainment of self-conscious personality, the individual is called upon to exercise his will and to choose for himself.

It is the time of dawning awareness of the world without, and of movement outwards in social relationships, when choices are inevitably demanded.

It is the time when, consciously or unconsciously, such choices are actually made, and character takes on that "set" which remains through life.

Thus, the *Encyclopædia of Religion and Ethics* says of middle adolescence that "religious conversion occurs more frequently during these years than at any other period of life."[30] Those youth organisations, too, which through Bible Classes, Camps, Missions or Campaigns, definitely appeal for decision for Christ, are rewarded with results that are quite remarkable, even in these days which are so difficult for young people.

206   As youth is the mirror of its age, and young people are the **Youth the** image and imprint of their generation, it is not surprising if they **mirror of** reflect the prevailing indifference of their elders to religion. Thus, **its age.** they require much evangelistic preparation before the Gospel can be personally presented to great numbers of them for their decision.

The decay of Christian home life has been disastrous. Present day parents, for the most part, while accepting the Christian ethic as an English inheritance, have paid scant attention to Christian worship. Their children (with the realism of youth) have interpreted non-attendance at church as a virtual denial of Christianity. The effect has been far reaching. Together with the Christian faith, the younger generation has jettisoned the assumptions on which moral behaviour rests. They still possess a sense of right and wrong but, as it is based on no clear view of life, it is uncertain; and uncertainty produces immorality.

The modern influences that educate youth, even more out of school than in school, have been increasingly materialistic in outlook.

29 Don Byrne in *Messer Marco Polo.*
30 Vol. vi, p. 448 (*Middle Adolescence*).

A whole generation has been suckled in agnosticism, and come to regard Christianity as an outworn creed.

The pagan atmosphere of the wider world is so pervasive, and the unbelief encountered in working life so prevailing, that boys and girls of school-leaving age, pitch-forked into the company of adults, put away Christian teaching with other childish things. Christian standards, too, inculcated in childhood, are naturally discarded when it is discovered that society in general does not act upon them.

The abnormality of the times has had an inevitable effect upon innocents born, bred and trapped in an era of upheaval and insecurity between two major wars. Even if their revolt against it all does not include Christianity which has failed to prevent the debacle, they can see in religion no relevance to life as they know it, and in life itself no ultimate meaning.

The same good material. 207   Yet, despite all adverse circumstance, the young people of to-day are far from indifferent to the claims of Christ. On the contrary there are indications that they are more than ever responsive to His call.

They are not impatient of authority, unless it is autocratic. Rather, conscious as they are of a lack of purpose and direction in life, they look for authority, and welcome it when it is harnessed to a worth-while purpose they can understand and in which they can share.

Hence, the wonderful response of the youth of the country to the discipline of war service, and the outstanding qualities of cheerful sacrifice which it has displayed.

The very considerable expansion of youth work during the war years offers the opportunity of directing this characteristic readiness for service into the highest channels, if it is seized by youth leaders who are convinced Christians. "There is no doubt that there is now a much higher proportion of young people associated with some form of training and service . . . than there has ever been before."[31]   In this connection it should be widely known that Confirmed members of the Church form an extraordinarily high percentage of the officers, N.C.O.'s and cadets of Pre-Service Units.

The big appeal. 208   Youth being what it is, it is the greatest mistake to seek to reduce the claims of Christianity, or its supernatural quality, to the " How much will Jones swallow? " criterion of some purveyors of respectable Christianity. Young Jones relishes a mouthful; any-

[31] *Teachers and Youth Leaders*, par. 337 (the McNair Report, H.M.S.O., 1944).

thing, in fact, rather than the Laodicean mixture offered him by far too many well-meaning club leaders.

It is the big demand, the absorbing cause, the hardest task, the Hero to worship, that captures the young, and wherein they find themselves and their Saviour. For example, the story of the Church on active service throughout the world is an appeal that is found to win their interest, leading to a full committal to Jesus Christ and to the service of His world-wide Church.

209 The opportunity afforded to the Church to-day of evangelising youth is almost unprecedented. Youth clubs, Pre-Service Units, and the proposed County Colleges, all present fruitful fields for evangelism, if only the Church will fully enter into them all. Through the influence of Christian members, and the provision of youth leaders, the Church can give these organizations essential assistance in that building up of character which is the declared purpose of the Service of Youth. **The opportunity to-day.**

In so doing, those who represent the Church to youth will have betrayed their trust if the young people who pass through their hands have not been confronted with the Person of the Living Christ, and so brought to the point of decision whether or no they will accept Him as Saviour and King, and serve Him in the fellowship of His Church.

210 Much experience has been accumulated as to the manifold methods that can be successfully employed to interest youth in religion, and to present the Gospel, indirectly, to young people. These have been dealt with in a Memorandum prepared by the Church of England Youth Council on " Evangelism and Youth." **The need of direct evangelism.**

We would, however, ask the Youth Council to give further attention to methods of direct evangelism, and also to the problem of leading on those who share in the religious activities of the youth organization into the worship and life of the Church.

211 The question is continually raised whether the Church is best advised to confine its energy to "closed" clubs, in which membership of the Church is a condition of membership of the club, or whether it should be responsible for open clubs having no such condition of membership. No hard and fast answer can be given. As agencies for evangelism, however, it can be stated that those clubs have proved successful in which there has been a percentage of open members, but not greater than the Church members could influence. **Church youth clubs.**

Training Youth to evangelise.

212 In any case, every church should possess its band of young people, training to evangelise their fellows. The young make grand evangelists of the young, and are most readily listened to by them. The time and pains devoted to such an inner circle are repaid with definite results that infinitely outweigh the same time and pains spent in running an open club.

APPENDED NOTE ON ECUMENICAL CO-OPERATION

In what follows on evangelism and ecumenical co-operation, the practical issue at the moment is the co-operation of the Church of England and the Free Churches in the task of evangelism. The co-operation of the Roman Communion is denied us. Co-operation with the Orthodox Church has no direct concern with the re-conversion of England.

Up to the present, evangelism in a divided Church tends to be confused by two opposing tendencies:—

1. *Evangelism is most commonly conducted on a purely denominational basis.* Since the issue of evangelism must be loyalty to an organised Church, it is natural for the evangelist to assume that the Church of his allegiance includes all that is necessary to salvation, and that it only complicates matters to try and explain Christian divisions to those outside.

2. *Evangelism is increasingly being attempted on an undenominational basis.* Many are so impressed by the menace of secularism, and so convinced that a national movement of evangelism must be on a united front, that they are willing to postpone distinctive church witness in order to present to those outside a general Christian agreement. The tendency has been noticeable (though often unconscious) in Religion and Life Campaigns, and in many informal acts of local witness.

The situation has been made more acute by the actions of some advocates of the undenominational method of evangelism, making advocates of the denominational method more intransigent. It is further complicated by two factors of great importance.

First, the weight of sheer indifference to evangelism, and the institutional rigidity characteristic of so many congregations, makes continued disunion easy even where it is not doctrinally necessary.

Secondly, there is the invasion of all denominations by a "liberalism" which advocates an easy and compromising tolerance, because it is chary of accepting Divine revelation.

The problem therefore is two-fold:—

(a) How are we to acknowledge those deep theological differences of doctrine and order, which brought a divided Christendom into existence in a passionate desire to safeguard revealed truth?

(b) At the same time, how are we to present to the world that common acknowledgment of the lordship of Christ which unites all the churches?

Here it is well to remember (more particularly in this age of change) that schism has not in fact occurred except when political, social or cultural forces coincided with doctrinal issues to cause it. The split between Western and Eastern churches coincided with the division of the Roman Empire. Protestant churches emerged with the rise of nationalism, Independency with the rise of the commercial middle class, Methodism with the rise of agrarian proletariat. Even the Salvation Army owes its origin to the submerged masses of industrial cities.

Similarly, in the other direction, if our age produces a powerful social drive towards uniformity (and there is every sign that it will) we must expect it to influence the divisions of Christendom. The danger is lest these social forces should compel a superficial unity only. Such a unity would combine all those whose grasp of Christian truth is slight. But it would drive all others into a series of "confessing minorities." These would still be divided by their understanding of Christian dogma. But they would be united in their refusal to be unified by Cæsar, and in their joint exclusion from a lawful status in society. The history of modern Germany and Japan is written for our warning.

THE ECUMENICAL MOVEMENT

There is only one way in which this dilemma can be avoided. A new and powerful co-operation must get to work, which is capable of controlling the drift towards secular unification, because it works from premises dictated by Christian faith and not by secular expediency. Is such a solution conceivable? *The Ecumenical Movement seems to be the answer.* The movement is dictated, not by the urgent practical considerations of evangelism (which may induce theologically unsound solutions), but by the very nature of the Church, as expressed in our Lord's high-priestly prayer for its unity. The late Archbishop described the movement as "the great new fact of our time." There is already a considerable body of experience of ecumenical work. It has been the mainspring of the Student Christian Movement, and of the World's Student Christian Federation. Its activity is evidenced in the International Missionary Council, the Faith and Order Movement, and in the Oxford Conference on Church, Community and State in 1937. Its latest development in this country has been the formation of the British Council of Churches.

We must now attempt some description of the Ecumenical Movement, both as regards its theological implications and its practical working.

THE THEOLOGICAL IMPLICATIONS OF THE ECUMENICAL MOVEMENT

In essence ecumenicity regards with full seriousness a fellow Christian of a separated church. It accepts him in Christ not in spite of, but *because* of, his allegiance to another church. It sees him, thereby, as reflecting Christ, not as an individual with different views, but as the bearer of a different church life. Thus (as found in practice) the first effect of ecumenical experience is to deepen and sharpen church-consciousness. But since it also deepens and sharpens the awareness of other churches *as* churches, it prohibits proselytising.

As such, ecumenical consciousness is essentially an experience peculiar to the *interior* life of the churches as they deal with one another. It is meaningless outside the Household of Faith. It is equally meaningless (though potentially not so) to a Christian who has only had a neutral, or a negative, attitude to fellow Christians of other churches. But for Christians who have ecumenical experience, evangelism shares the same paradox as contact between Christians.

A much fuller discussion of the theological implications of this attitude is to be found in a pamphlet *Mouvement Ecumenique*[32]. The main point made by the writer is that *every* Christian is what he is, not as an isolated individual but because he has been born and nurtured in some great tradition. In that tradition he both bears Christ, and witnesses to Christ. "*Christophoria* becomes *Christophania*: such is the brief formula which defines the essence of the ecumenical process." That is why no Christian can ignore the fellow-Christian of another tradition without ignoring a witness to Christ.

H

Christians can thus co-operate to draw men into any one of the churches, knowing that the convert (once he is in any church) must also be made to face the fact of ecumenical experience, namely, the anomalous dis-unity-within-unity which is the characteristic of a divided Christendom, in which men have put asunder what God joined.

THE PRACTICAL WORKING OF THE ECUMENICAL MOVEMENT

In contemporary England evangelism will often mean restoring to a man the full apprehension of his own neglected church tradition. Where (as will sometimes and increasingly happen) there is no neglected church loyalty to be restored, the individual evangelist must speak out of the fulness of his own church tradition. But he will do so in company with colleagues from other churches who will not grudge him the right to do so, for they do the same.

It may be objected that such a proceeding is only to confuse the convert. We can only reply that the divisions of Christendom have already confused him. The advantage of the practice is that evangelism is being done by agents who have faced and transcended the confusions imposed by division, in so far as they can be transcended short of Christian unity being restored. Those, for example, who have spoken at an S.C.M. Conference to a group of students of all traditions and of none, and accompanied by fellow speakers of other traditions, will have some ex-perience of how this can be effectively done in practice.

What particular church the convert may join, is the responsibility of the Holy Ghost alone. It is enough for the evangelists that each has borne his witness without compromising his own convictions or concealing the divisions of Christendom. Such further problems as inter-communion are not relevant to the ecumenical method as such. They are part of the church tradition of the various churches, and thus become part of the intractable material on which the ecumenical method must work.(33)

SUMMARY

Evangelism in a divided church can only be conducted on one of three grounds:—

1. *The ignoring of divided fellow Christians.* The results are (or often may be) arrogance in ourselves, and the inducing of a similar arrogance in our converts. We deny the reality of Christ's presence in other Christian bodies when we speak *to the world* as though Christ had no other witnesses.

2. *The ignoring of vital dogmatic differences.*(34) This is to betray the integrity of those who bore us in Christ. It is, also, a betrayal of our converts; for it is to admit them to less than the full, paradoxical, nature of the Church's heritage.

3. *The Ecumenical Method.* This pre-supposes, for its effective employ-ment, agents who have some ecumenical experience. Accordingly, all churches would make the fullest possible use, in their evangelism, of those who already have some experience of ecumenical work. They would, also, continually train new agents, both centrally(35) and in their congregations.

Sometimes, in a given situation, it may be necessary to choose between denominational and undenominational evangelism. If so (as we have noted) the exaggeration of the one leads by reaction to an exaggeration of the other. It is vital to realise that a third possibility exists. It is also vital to have our eyes open to which of the other two methods we are employing, lest we confuse both ourselves and our converts. If the Ecumenical Method itself is not to degenerate into undenominationalism, it calls for continuous integrity, training and a critical self-awareness; none of which is at present widespread.

Finally, the Church of England has a unique position of possible leadership in the Ecumenical Movement. The Church of England bears within its own body the main constituents of creative ecumenical conflict, namely the co-existence of the Catholic tradition and of the insights of the Reformation. For the Church of England to fulfil its own nature would be, in itself, to exhibit the beginning of ecumenical evangelism.

---

[32] By. Prof. L. Zander of the Russian Orthodox Church (published by the Priory of Amay-sur-Meuse). The greater part of the pamphlet is translated in the Student World (Second Quarter, 1937).

[33] See the pamphlet issued by the Secretariat of the *Faith and Order Conference* reviewing "the rules and customs of churches concerning inter-communion and open communion.

[34] Needless to say, differences must be *vital* if their ignoring is too serious. But the discernment of whether they are vital is a part of the ceaseless ecumenical convergence itself.

[35] Cf. the Commission on Training for the Ministry, p. 70, par. 136(b) on *Hawarden*.

CHAPTER V

EVANGELISM. PREPARING FOR THE GOSPEL

"It must be remembered that when exhortation and suggestion are at variance, suggestion always wins. Christians must take their part in re-creating a sound social and cultural life, and thereby healing the modern divided consciousness, in which head and heart have become divorced and man's conscious purposes are no longer in harmony with the forces which give direction and tone to their emotional life."
                                                                    WILLIAM TEMPLE.

The two stages in evangelism. IN evangelism we have distinguished two stages, though their operation is, generally, contemporary rather than successive.

In the previous chapter we dealt with the one stage of the direct and personal presentation of the Gospel for decision.

Preceding, or concurrent with, the stage of direct appeal, there must always be the other stage of preparing for the Gospel. It is the more indirect and impersonal approach of arousing interest, teaching eternal truths, and showing their relevance to life.

In Bible analogy the two stages correspond to preparing the soil and sowing the seed.

Preparing for the Gospel. 214   A strong desire for anything must be preceded by the consciousness of a want. Before people long for a change in their present condition, they must have become dissatisfied with that condition. He who embarks upon a certain course of action, must first be satisfied that it is at least relevant to the supplying of his need.

If, therefore, Christ Jesus is *so* to be presented to men that they will have ears to hear, and *desire* to accept Him as Saviour and King, they must first be enabled to feel their *need* for the Gospel. So it was that in the so-called Parable of the Sower, our Lord stressed the importance of the quality of the soil, and showed, thereby, the need to soften the hardness of indifference, to deepen the shallowness of complacency, and to out-root alien influences which stifle belief.

Normal methods of preparation. 215   *Informal Discussion* has already proved one of the most effective educative forces for penetrating the prevailing religious indifference of our day and generation. By its informality and fearless operation the mental subsoil is loosened, and a softening process introduced which breaks down intellectual barriers to the reception of the Gospel.

The Proclamation of Eternal Truths is the prophetic method (of which Scripture is the record) for shattering the apathy of complacency, by awakening conscience to the fact of God, and arousing reason to explore spiritual reality. We cannot lay too great emphasis on the importance of prophetic preaching once again proclaiming from every pulpit in the land, "Thus saith the Lord."

Christian Social Witness must ceaselessly strive so to shape the temporal order that its social structure, and the pattern of men's lives, shall conform with their Christian aims and beliefs, and thus express the Kingdom of God.

216   All these three methods of preparation for the reception of the Gospel—teaching, preaching, and social witness—must be constantly operative. They form essential features in the evangelistic ministry of an ordinary parish, as we shall show in the next chapter. *Special methods of preparation.*

But for their effective functioning in these days of mass suggestion, and of highly developed and scientific devices for communicating ideas, it is also necessary to use to the full all those great cultural forces of propaganda which now, more than any other influence, mould the mental habit of men and give shape to their emotions.

We, therefore, devote this chapter to a consideration of the employment of these modern agencies for the purposes of evangelism, and to the possibilities of Christian education by means of organised advertising.

MODERN AGENCIES OF PROPAGANDA

IN the world of to-day the main influences in the lives of our people in their mechanistic environment, and largely affecting their attitude to religion and the Church, are secular. Unless the realisation of this fact touches motive and creates energetic action, the growth of secularism and the decay of church-going may both increase. *New methods of evangelism.*

Owing to the shortage of priests, parish ministries are rarely more than holding operations among the few. Missions, too, even of the modern variety, fall, for the most part, into the same category. Their appeal is almost exclusively to those who have not entirely lost the habit of worship.

The initial stage of preparation for evangelism cannot now be attempted on a large scale unless the Church uses those media which mould men's convictions—the cinema, drama, radio, television, the Press, popular literature, and the whole field of organised advertising. Must the Church abdicate from these powerful means of propaganda, and relinquish them, with their all-pervasive influence, to the forces of secularism?

Should the Church employ them? *218* The question will be raised whether the Church ought to follow the methods employed by the world in "conditioning" men's minds. "Surely," it will be said, "the Church's principle must ever be to seek from men a rational assent to the Gospel." The answer is that the purpose of the Church in thus using modern agencies of propaganda would be educational, and to counteract the weight of wholly secular suggestion which they now bring to bear upon our people. Man would always remain free to choose, but the choice would have been put before him.

Three possible courses. *219* The further question then arises as to the policy the Church should adopt in order to use these modern methods for the work of evangelism. There are three possible courses, none of which excludes the use of the other two.

1. The Church might enter the field of these agencies on its own account : starting its own paper, running its own theatre, producing its own films.

2. Or the Church might seek to permeate and influence the great corporations that control these forces.

3. Or, again, the Church might employ its own agencies, but by way rather of supplementation than of competition, encouraging and strengthening those it already possesses, and revolutionising its own religious papers and periodicals.

The right method, or methods, can only be discovered by experiment and enterprise, and by following up resolutely any opening that may offer.

Only the best in God's service. *220* On one point, however, the Commission was agreed. In the use of these modern agencies only the best art and technique can be offered by the Church for the glory and service of God. As with the great religious art and music of the past, the first consideration is not the piety of the producer but the perfection of the production. It is with the conviction that whatever media of modern propaganda the Church employs, it must not fall short of the highest professional standards, we now examine the possibilities of some of them.

1. THE CINEMA

221   There does not exist one technically satisfactory religious film which is the work of the Church. There are religious films, commercially produced, which Christians ought to see and which strengthen the Christian cause, such as *Green Pastures*. But none appeared on the screen with any evangelistic intention. Broadly speaking (and acknowledging the work of religious film societies) the Church has made no effective effort to use this most powerful agency to evangelise the nation.

Unused by the Church.

Yet against some five million attendances at church each week, there are some forty million attendances at cinemas. The disparity is much greater among the young. The cinema for many is the most powerful medium for conveying ideas and elevating, or debasing, thought and conduct. If we exclude the word "debasing," the achievement of the cinema is not an inaccurate description of the purpose of the Church.

222   The work of religious film societies should be given more support by the Church. Much may be done in parishes with sub-standard films,[1] and those which treat of Bible stories, lives of saints and missionary work. But they hardly touch the problem of evangelism, and that for two reasons:—

Religious film societies.

1.   They give the impression that Christianity is something belonging in the past.

2.   They are amateurish, slight and produced for the parish hall; not for the commercial cinema where non-worshippers congregate.

223   The Church should occupy a central place in Wardour Street as it does in Broadcasting House. The Church's message should be shown and spoken in the cinemas of the country.

The objective.

It will be objected that the Church has not the money to compete with the big film companies. True, but there are two facts to be borne in mind:—

(1)   Good films make profits. They do not lose money. *The Song of Bernadette* was immensely costly, but it will bring immense profits; and its public appeal is shown in the fact that already several million adults have paid to see it. The Church has a story to tell

---

[1] 16 and 8 millimetres.

which can be told in innumerable films better, professionally, than *Bernadette,* and be just as remunerative.

(2) The greatest and most lasting films (such as *Carnet de Bal,* made by the small capital of the actors) are the cheapest. A film which is technically and professionally good will always make money.

A policy. 224   Moreover, the best policy may well be for the Church to be in the film world, suggesting themes and offering stories, even as it is in the B.B.C. There is evidence that Wardour Street would welcome such a development. People want good religious films.

But there is no one as yet in the cinema industry to suggest the right themes, or to guide, theologically and religiously, the script writer and film director. *A Canterbury Tale* is a recent example of a brilliant producer being given a poor story.

The first step. 225   The immense opportunity presented by the cinema makes it urgently important that there should be set up a strong committee of experts, composed of professional artists and directors. It would advise the Church how to carry its message to the people through the art of the film. More especially do we need advice on the production of documentary films, in which England leads the world. They are admirably fitted for the work of evangelism.

2.   DRAMA

A revival of religious drama. 226   The drama, religious in origin, and the handmaid of the Church for centuries, is slowly regaining its position as an evangelistic agency. There are manifest signs of a renaissance of religious drama (as evidenced by the work of the Religious Drama Society and kindred bodies) which merit fuller support and recognition.

A policy. 227   But more is needed. The Church should be in Shaftesbury Avenue as in Wardour Street. The production of such plays as *Murder in the Cathedral* and *The Zeal of Thy House,* shows how the Church might call dramatists to the task of interpreting its message, professionally presented in a commercial theatre. Here again a permanent, and professionally strong, advisory committee would be a necessity.

Parish Plays. 228   Miracle plays, and similar productions, are becoming increasingly a parochial activity. In order to save such evangelism

by drama from the well-meaning amateur, and people from plays
which have a good message but are bad art, steps might well be
taken to see that expert advice is available in every diocese.

229   Evangelism through religious drama will not achieve its **Consecra-**
full purpose, nor avoid the dangers which face the acting profes- **tion.**
sion, unless the whole venture is prepared for by prayer and
dedication and is the expression of a religious faith. Though all
the piety in the world cannot compensate for bad drama, nor for
bad acting and production, yet *Selzach* and *Oberammergau* are
constant reminders of the evangelistic power of technical excellence
wedded to genuine piety.

3. RADIO

230   Of the modern agencies of propaganda, only broadcasting **History of**
has been at all adequately used by the Church. To-day, religious **religious**
broadcasting is, perhaps, the greatest power for indirect evangelism **broad-**
offered to the Church. **casting.**

    The history of religious broadcasting is instructive. The
original desire and drive for religious broadcasting came from the
B.B.C. The only opposition (and it was at times very great) came
from the Church. Will history repeat itself when television enters
every home?

231   The Church in Broadcasting House can only rise to the **Broadcast-**
height of its evangelistic opportunity in proportion as it receives the **ing House**
fullest co-operation from the Church in the parish. Their ministries **and the**
are complementary the one to the other. Religious broadcasting **parish**
must be recognised as the work of the Church. Those responsible **church.**
for religious broadcasting are the servants of the Church in Broadcasting House. Religious broadcasting, with its immense resources
and its annihilation of space, is able to take the Gospel into every
home in the land. It is the Church in one activity, even as parochial work is the Church in another. In this connection we make
three observations.

232   First, apart from bringing religious services and teaching **Evangelism.**
to those who cannot attend a place of worship, the true task of
religious broadcasting is missionary and evangelistic. The Church
looks to it to reach those who can, but do not, attend church. But
as religious broadcasting cannot exert a sacramental and pastoral
ministry, it can only plough the land and sow the seed. It is for
the Church in its parochial aspect to tend and reap.

Education. *233*   Secondly, after the war, with parochial co-operation, the powerful medium of religious broadcasting can be harnessed to a nation-wide campaign of serious adult religious education. The Church in the parish can organise listening and discussion groups, and the Church in the B.B.C. can provide the teachers.

Worship. *234*   Thirdly, religious broadcasting (apart from its ministry to those who cannot attend church) aims increasingly at expressing itself in terms of its own medium, not at reflecting normal church services. Church worship was never meant to be an experience of sound only. Such an aim will involve research, thinking and experiment by the Church, if broadcasting is to find out the equivalent in sound of the actions and symbols we use in church. It will also mean meeting and overcoming the dangers, which certainly now exist, of easy religion, irreverence and individualism.

Religious broadcasting should not attempt what churches can do better. *The Man born to be King* showed the Church using the microphone properly. But for the microphone, these plays could not have been written, acted or heard. Religious broadcasting has increasingly to learn how to use its own medium properly.

4. TELEVISION

Its mighty influence. *235*   It is said by those who know best that television will be in nearly every home in the land in ten or fifteen years. It is impossible to estimate what may be the power of suggestion exerted by television. It might conceivably become the greatest single influence on the minds and lives of our people, exceeding the power of radio, film or the Press.

The study of its use an urgent task. *236*   With the contrast of the cinema and radio before us as spiritual influences, will the Church realise *now* the potentialities of television, and take immediate action?

The task is immense. Religious broadcasting is easy compared with religious television. The Church is faced with creating an entirely new technique of preaching the Gospel through the medium of television, and of preaching it every day.

As yet, no work has been done on this matter, no research, no thinking. But how shall the people hear without a preacher? That means a preacher in television, as well as in radio, the Press and so on. How can the Church hope to preach the Gospel to *every* creature, unless the Church preaches in the media to which the the people will attend?

Television presents the Church with a real challenge. Before television begins again (a matter of months only, it may be) the Church must act. One of the first tasks of the Council for Evangelism we recommend will be the setting up of a Commission on Television consisting of technical experts in the use of television, and specialists in modern methods of evangelism.[2]

5. THE PRESS

237 In the newspaper press the Church has ready at hand an instrument of immense value, but it is slow in making proper use of it. Nowadays, when every Government Department and almost all public bodies and commercial corporations find it necessary to maintain a public relations organisation, it may properly be asked why the Church appears to attach little importance to such work. The provision made by the Church Assembly for the work of the Press and Publications Board is woefully inadequate. It is highly creditable to the very small staff employed that so much good work is done in supplying the press with a regular daily news service, a weekly service of notes and news for country papers, and much information in answer to inquiries; as well as watching the periodical press generally and endeavouring to correct mis-statements. *The Press and Publications Board.*

238 The number of dioceses which possess an efficient press organisation can be counted on the fingers of one hand. The distaste for any suspicion of publicity seems deep-seated. A principal difficulty which the Press Bureau of the Press and Publications Board encounters is that of extracting news from the dioceses. Few dioceses have any competent internal organisation for good relations with their own local Press. Most dioceses remain unco-operative. *Diocesan organisations.*

239 Though the Press is friendly to the Church of England, it is not so circumspect towards it as it is towards some other religious bodies, notably the Roman Catholic Church and the Christian Science organisation, which exercise expert vigilance. Every journalist knows, also, that he can be sure of full and courteous attention at Archbishop's House, Westminster. It is understood that one of the aims of Hinsley House, the proposed memorial to Cardinal Hinsley, is better provision for the Press. At Lambeth he may, or may not, find someone to answer his inquiry; and the Press and Publications Board office closes at the hour when newspaper offices are most active. *Fleet St.*

2 See Recommendation, par. 363.

It is the exception for a newspaper office of any size not to have among its staff a Roman Catholic sufficiently well-informed on ecclesiastical affairs to see to it that his paper does not make stupid blunders and that Roman Catholic news is not neglected. Rome has for long recognised the importance of an apostolate of the press. We have barely begun to think in such terms. We ought to foster vocations to journalism and, by such means, ally the power of the press to the work of evangelism. At present even the Church press is amateurish.

Liaison with the press.

240   A beginning has, however, been made with Press Conferences designed to give journalists background information on Church affairs. This technique should be extended, but calls for a public relations service which cannot at present be rendered by the Press and Publications Board. There is urgent need for some sort of Press attaché in the confidence of an Archbishop or Bishop. He should be a man in Holy Orders and of some standing. The press is accustomed to be taken into the confidence of ministers and high officials of Government. For example, there are daily military press conferences at the Ministry of Information, and (before the war) there were weekly press conferences at the Foreign Office. At such conferences any question is permissible, though not all answers are for publication.

The press blunders over Church affairs to the great irritation of many readers, mainly because it is kept in the dark about what is happening. Journalists are used to keeping political and military secrets; they are seldom trusted with Church secrets. They ought to be able to turn to a personal representative of the Primate, with knowledge of newspaper needs, for trustworthy information and guidance and for "background."

The clergy and reporters.

241   The parochial clergy can exercise great influence on the Press, owing to the fact that very many of them can come into contact with young journalists at the outset of their careers, when serving as "cub reporters" on small country weeklies. The Church provides a large proportion of the news for such papers, and a life-long friend of the Church may be made by the assistance which a clergyman gives to a young man or woman who is new to the job, sensitive to rebuff, and probably a little bumptious by way of psychological compensation. On the other hand, a life-long animosity to the Church, coming out in perhaps no more than the turn of a phrase or a caption under a photograph, may be traced to

brusque treatment in impressionable years by a self-important incumbent or rural dean.

A Church newspaper.

242 The question of a distinctly Church paper, comparable with *La Croix* or the *Christian Science Monitor* must be weighed. It is virtually impossible to launch a new daily with smaller capital than £1,000,000, but it might be possible to acquire an influential shareholding in an existing publication.

A less ambitious project would be a weekly paper not exclusively devoted to purely ecclesiastical affairs. Something of the intellectual quality and excellence of the *New Statesman,* conducted with a Christian outlook, is needed. It would have to command the best brains to put over the Christian apologetic. We have to reach the secular world of young civil servants, school and university teachers, and the politically minded of both sexes. Such a paper would aim at recovering respect for the Christian religion and become a powerful antagonist of secular philosophies. It is true that converts are not usually made by argument, but at present the case for Christianity goes by default. The ordinary newspaper reader quite genuinely believes that there is nothing that the adult mind need bother itself with in Christianity, which he regards as an historic survival.

Local newspapers.

243 The opportunity for evangelism afforded by local newspapers is not sufficiently grasped nor utilised. Space for religious articles in local papers is generally given on a generous scale, and well written news items of current church happenings are always welcomed. Then, be it remembered that *most people read every word of their local paper*.

A missed opportunity.

244 The Church is not press-minded and, while the Press is on the whole civil to the Church, it is less and less inclined to give positive support to the Christian view. Its reports are noncommital; its comments rare and faintly patronising. Herein is discernible proprietorial influence, and it will not be remedied until the Church shows itself willing to take much more responsibility for the use of the newspaper press. An address by Mr. Henry Martin, editor in chief of the Press Association, to provincial editors last year, should be read in this connection.[3]

3 *The Place of Religion in the Post-war Press*, price 6d. C.A. Press and Publications Board, 2 Gt. Peter St., Westminster, S.W.1.

6. LITERATURE

A first claim upon the Church. 245   The literature available for purposes of evangelism is totally inadequate. Most religious books and pamphlets are designed for the converted. In style and language they would neither attract, nor be understood, by the great mass of people outside the Church.

The value of the printed page cannot be too strongly emphasized. The production of attractive, well-produced and cheap literature intended for non-worshippers, constitutes a first claim upon the Church. The fact, however, must be stressed that such literature, to be effective, must be up-to-date and compare favourably with that published for secular purposes.

What is required. 246   The literature required for evangelism falls into two main categories, namely, literature for evangelism, the purpose of which would be to bring the Christian message to others; and literature on evangelism, of which the purpose would be to teach the technique of evangelism, and to instruct evangelists in the Christian faith and life.

I. LITERATURE FOR EVANGELISM

Periodicals. 247   The scope is so wide that we can do no more than mention three main types of literature for evangelism.

Monthly periodicals are called for which would arrest and challenge, as well as interest, the casual reader who purchased them at a railway bookstall. A religious *Weekly Digest* is called for. A religious *Picture Post* is also needed, or something of the *Lilliput* variety, to give a pictorial news survey of the work of the world-wide Church.

Pamphlets. 248   *Pamphlets and leaflets* are increasingly becoming important instruments of propaganda. Effective work has been done in the past by the old-fashioned tract. When brought up to date, there is complete unanimity as to the value of this type of literature.

Different types of pamphlets are needed. Some would deal with the relevance of the faith to modern problems, and explain the Christian attitude on a wide range of subjects. Others would treat, non-technically, various aspects of the Christian faith, thus providing a certain amount of instruction. Others again would present the challenge of Christ, and show the meaning of personal faith, and the way thereto. The four-page leaflet is also of value, especially for free distribution.

In them all, modern production, drawings, and (in some cases) cartoons, will be essential to arrest the interest of the casual reader. The public now expect current phraseology and arresting lay-out in all forms of literature. Anything put out by the Church which does not come up to such a standard, will not only be useless, but prove a real hindrance by confirming the widely held view that the Church is out of date.

249   *Books on the Christian faith,* but of a non-technical type, **Books.** and similar to the Penguin books in size, price and get-up, would be widely read and in unexpected quarters. The great publishing houses are ready, and even anxious, to publish religious books. The chief requirement is a far closer liaison between them and the Church.

Text-books on secular subjects (science, politics, economics, social problems), but with a Christian basis, and produced cheaply, would prove an adjunct to evangelism of the greatest possible value. They should be written by foremost scholars and experts who are Christians, though they would contain no definite reference to Christianity. The Christian faith of the writers would impregnate the material, in the same way as does the agnosticism of the writers of such books as those published in the *Thinkers' Library*. Writing of this Mr. C. S. Lewis says: "No evangelism can have wide success against the continual glut of cheap scientific books written on atheistic principles. . . . The little books are regarded as intellectual. We must remedy the situation in which the working man, wishing to learn a little about biology, economics or geology, always finds that the cheapest (or only) literature is by an atheist. We need *œuvres de vulgarisation* by Christians, with their Christianity latent (that is essential) . . . We must attack on the enemy's lines of communication."[4]

2. LITERATURE ON EVANGELISM

250   As our bibliography shows,[5] there is a great dearth of books and pamphlets designed to give instruction on the principles and technique of evangelism to those engaged in, or training for, the work.

Such literature is repeatedly asked for by the clergy and must continue to be an urgent need. Moreover, as we have previously indicated,[6] the training of the laity in evangelism will demand manuals and text books. They would deal with the understanding

4 From a letter to the Chairman.
5 See page 157.
6 See par. 144.

and application of psychological principles in evangelism, the handling of personal problems, the use of the Bible in individual work, modern methods of approach, as well as with Christian doctrine and current intellectual difficulties.

7. CHRISTIAN INFORMATION AND PUBLICITY CENTRES

A mood of enquiry.

251   There is evidence of a mood of enquiry with regard to religion in the minds of the general public. The popularity of Brains Trusts, Padres' Hours, Religion and Life Weeks; the increase in the numbers of those who listen to the religious broadcasts; the spontaneous coming together of small groups in factories and business premises for religious purposes; all testify to an evident interest in religion. It is a paradoxical situation, seeing that there has been a general retreat from organised religion.

This is significant. Among persons of all ages and classes, and in unexpected as well as expected places, there seem to be latent resources of goodwill, loyalty and enthusiasm. How can these be claimed and enlisted in Christian service? At present they are largely dammed up behind a wall of ignorance, prejudice and inertia; so that only the smallest trickle seeps through into the recognised channels. To meet the situation, experiments are being made with Christian Information and Publicity Centres. We have here a movement that should be encouraged to grow and spread, rather than to be imposed or organised on a big and general scale.

The use of publicity centres.

252   Such local publicity centres, as have already come into existence, fulfil three functions. They provide: —

(1)   *A headquarters* for local Christian bodies. Preferably a shop is taken with windows for the display of posters and literature, and possessing rooms for committees and meetings.

(2)   *A bureau* for dealing with enquiries and personal problems, after the manner of the *Citizens' Advice Bureau.*

(3)   *A propaganda centre and book room,* deliberately designed to appeal to that enquiring multitude who are interested, but will not at present, go to church.

THE POSITION REVIEWED.

The past conquests of the Church.

253   In its great ages the Catholic Church has claimed its place and God's sovereignty in every activity of life. The early Church did not only outlive classical humanism, it also out-thought it. The Church has been the pioneer in education, in hospital work, in philanthropy. The Church led the way in social reform, and the abolition of slavery. The Church informed, inspired and perfected architecture, painting, music, literature and drama. But what of to-day? It helplessly watches the forces of secularism, and sometimes the forces of evil, capture the powerful agencies of the cinema, the Press and the like. Only in radio can the Church in this country claim to have taken its place, and that imperfectly.

254   Nothing less will meet the case than a missionary invasion **A new missionary movement.** of the modern agencies of propaganda, so that we may claim and use them for Christ. But for such a missionary invasion there are two requirements:—

1. The first is to secure the means by which the Church can offer **Expert advice.** opportunities to artists and writers to use their gifts to an evangelistic end. Though advisory committees, such as we propose, can do nothing to create art or letters, they can provide that technical and professional expertness without which the Church's efforts would be incompetent and amateur—in all these spheres of influence "succeed or get out" is the law. They are also necessary in order to relate artistic and literary ability to avowed evangelism.

2. The other requirement is revived parish churches. If men **Revival.** hear the Gospel through the media to which they listen, they will be inevitably moved to turn to the Church. What will they find?

Any forward missionary movement using these agencies of modern propaganda for evangelism must go hand in hand with revival in our parishes.

THE CHURCH'S USE OF ADVERTISING

OF the eight agencies of propaganda we have mentioned, **What Experts say.** advertising is the only one about which we have obtained expert opinion. It is, also, the one which most people would hesitate to ask the Church to employ. We, therefore, print at some length the advice offered us, almost unsought, by eminent practitioners professionally engaged in the successful publicity of Government departments and commercial industries. We are deeply grateful to them; and would emphasise that similar expert and professional advice would as eagerly be placed at the disposal of the Church if it decided to use any of the other seven agencies.

The Technique of Advertising

The Government and advertising. 256   The Ministry of Food, H.M. Treasury, the Ministry of Information (the last acting for the Ministry of Health, the Board of Trade and the Ministry of Agriculture and Fisheries, among others) nowadays inform the public on various urgent matters with the persistence commonly displayed by commercial advertisers when they wish to be assured that the largest possible public will understand what they are saying.

The advertising arts are appropriately adapted to assure this public recognition of facts and acceptance of suggestion. They are not applied haphazardly, but selected, fashioned and co-ordinated with great care. For the desire is not only to move the public to act, but also to raise the public's estimate of the advertiser. That is to say, advertising is employed to educate the public up to an appreciation of the advertiser's aim.

The Minister of Agriculture has said: "Advertisements by Government departments in the Press represent a new element in our machinery of government, and as a medium of education they are probably unexcelled."

Public regard. 257   Government advertising, conducted as it is by separate departments, or through the Ministry of Information, not only succeeds in its prime aim, but also redounds to the credit of the department and of the Government.

As advertising would not be continued did it not bring the practical results, perhaps it would be of interest here to say something of the less obvious achievement in *prestige*.

The facts of long and wide experience prove two things:

First, public regard for an advertiser grows as he takes the public into his confidence.

Secondly, all engaged, no matter in what capacity, in producing and distributing what is advertised, tend to make it a point of pride to live up to the claims made.

A Government example. 258   The Ministry of Food has made it a basis of its policy to understand the emotions and experience of the individual. As well as disseminating information regarding each person's right to given quantities of certain foods and how to obtain them, it has used

Advertising to make known to the ordinary housewife its understanding of her difficulties, and to help her to surmount them. Thereby, the Ministry confronted with the most unpopular task of the war, has become one of the most widely respected of them all.

The Public Relations Officer of the Ministry of Food said recently: "We in the Ministry have watched with great interest the working out of this experiment of having weekly very personal, very human, advertisements. My advertising colleagues, of course, give all the credit to the Ministry's policy, but we know, both in the Public Relations Division and in the rest of the Ministry, what a great deal of research and creative thought goes into putting over that sort of message. I think, if I may say so, that it is a fine tribute to all concerned that Press advertising has been made in this way such a powerful and tactful servant of a Government Department."

259   An adequate advertising compaign exerts a strong unifying influence. Advertisers are invariably encouraged by the integration apparent as campaigns gather impetus. And in addition to a drawing together and pulling together of the known human agencies with those of the Press, posters, films, literature, lectures, and information bureaux, all these are augmented by various voluntary contributions from unexpected quarters. Moreover, every special local effort benefits from the national Press distributed in the district. It provides an otherwise unobtainable platform on which to base parochial appeals. *(The unifying influence of advertising.)*

There is no doubt about the immediate success of these modern methods both for practical results and raising prestige.

260   None of these advantages would be possible without an expertly organised campaign of educational advertising; for the unique and principal reason for its success is Repetition. While news columns open but once to a story, and even then usually not as completely as desired, reiteration of a carefully prepared message is possible in the advertisement columns. *(Repetition, the unique merit.)*

Only by saying over and over again what it is desired the public should grasp, can there be any confidence that the message is finding its mark.

261   We British are a newspaper reading public. Practically every household takes one or more newspapers daily, including Sundays. Twelve to sixteen million copies of newspapers are sold daily; in addition there is a large weekly journal and magazine *(Organised advertising.)*

press. Organised advertising—the advertisement columns of these newspapers, periodicals and magazines, together with other proved media—alone offers the required means of repetition.

Thereby you buy the space, can say what you like in it; and you can repeat your message as frequently and with the precise emphasis, and from as many angles as you desire.

ADVERTISING THE GOSPEL

Evangelism by advertising. *262*   The Government departments quoted above have followed industrialists in recognising the powers of Press advertising, co-ordinated with the use of posters, pamphlets, cinema films, information bureaux and the like. How can this method be applied to evangelism?

Dr. J. W. Welch, the Director of Religious Broadcasting of the B.B.C., has recently alluded to the "spiritual hunger of the people." He said: "There are millions of people who are not attached to any religious body but who habitually, day by day, listen to religious broadcasts and hold sincere Christian convictions. . . . Your eyes would be opened if you saw the mail week by week, and read some of the letters from lonely, spiritually starved people whose souls have been quickened by what has been said on the radio, and who have been out of touch with religion for many years."

Presenting the Gospel, *263*   We start with the assumption that it is always within the power of creative and inspired writing to interpret the Eternal Gospel in the idiom of the day in which we live. Given the message, all will agree that ways should be found to make it known.

in terms of to-day. *264*   Here let us repeat our definition of Evangelism:—
" To evangelise is so to present Jesus Christ in the power of the Holy Spirit that men shall come to put their trust in God through Him, to accept Him as their Saviour, and serve Him as their King in the fellowship of His church."[6]
In terms consonant with the "prevailing intellectual outlook of the non-worshipping members of the community,"[7] the objects of the kind of campaign we have in mind are:—
To make real to more people the idea of an inner life common to mankind;
and the presence and power of God with the individual who opens his heart to Him.

6 See par. 1   7 See *Terms of Reference*, p. v.

Further, to make better known those historic facts of Christianity which give the highest authority to this idea and point the way to this experience.

265   In the advertisement columns of the Press we have a vehicle **Advertising campaigns.** for a modern form of tract. By it a message can be carried into almost every household over and over again, and in ways whereby the millions of readers must eventually see it and grasp something of its meaning.

The plan of campaign would be shaped by the need for reading-space sufficient for the argument, and for frequent reminders so that the idea can hardly be overlooked by the reading public.

Sunday newspapers, weekly journals and magazines, are not quickly discarded, but remain at hand for days or weeks, perhaps in a family circle, before they are passed to, or exchanged with, other readers similarly placed. They therefore provide the opportunity for *leisurely reflection.*

The public are best *reminded* by morning and evening newspapers, posters and the two-minute cinema films; and by those even shorter films, similar to the "Food Flashes" made popular by the Ministry of Food during the war.

266   A plan of campaign to apply educational propaganda to the **A plan.** mission of evangelism, would include the following items:—

A call to prayer on this sustained effort to apply educational propaganda to the service of evangelism.

The B.B.C.

Special sermons.

Repetition of their special message through all advertising media.

Editorial support.

Public meetings in London and simultaneous meetings through the country.

Repetition of their special message through all advertising media.

Regional conferences of church social groups.

Public meetings.

Subsequent advertisements on selected themes.

Extensions by pamphlets and books.

267   As some central organisation will be needed to execute a **A central office.** co-ordinated plan of campaign, we suggest, as an interim

expedient, the addition of a Publicity Department to the Press and Publications Board of the Church Assembly. Steps will also have to be taken to cope with the correspondence, which will be heavy and often critical.

Personal dealings.

268 Mass education always throws forward individuals for personal treatment. Any forward movement, such as we have outlined above, will demand the existence of revivified churches, of small groups of church members preparing themselves as contacts—the Good Neighbours on the look-out for enquirers, and of local Publicity Centres.[8]

THE COST

An estimate.

269 We foresee the need to assess the total cost over a long period covered by a series of successive and accumulative campaigns; for it is not to be expected that anything approaching the maximum achievement can be effected in less than, say, a generation.

The first stage we envisage as a Five Years Development Campaign. The expenditure on this, as on that in subsequent years, should have some relationship to the importance and need of the work. The Ministry of Food spends in Press and poster advertising alone something in the region of £500,000 a year. Even more is spent in the Savings Campaign. In peace-time, the largest commercial campaigns range about £300,000 a year, and there are campaigns estimated to cost half-million a year.

An evangelistic campaign for the re-conversion of England is of infinitely greater importance than any of these. But it would be extravagant and wasteful to attempt to force the pace by the expenditure of anything like these sums of money at the outset.

We are advised that the cost of this first Five Years Campaign proposal should develop to the rate of about £200,000 a year; and by the end of the first year of its inception the expenditure might reach half that amount.

Resources.

270 The provision of the money required to meet the cost of such a continuous integrating and developing effort in evangelism would

8 See pars. 92, 122, 148, 251, 254.

NOTE.—On the opposite page is an illustration of what might be done. Decision as to theme, phrasing and design would be the responsibility of the Publicity Committee of the Press and Publications Board which we have suggested.

NOW

CONGRESS heard from Mr. Joseph Vian, president of the Butchers' organisation, that butchers in New Jersey were starting 7 meat-eases.

"They are already starting to put venetian blinds in the windows," added.

NO-MEAT MEAT LUNCH

MEAT was not on the menu for the luncheon in London yesterday of the Association of Multiple Retail Meat Traders, who had as chief guest Mr. Mabane, Parliamentary Secretary to the Food Ministry.

They had hors d'œuvre (sardines, smoked herring and rollmops), boiled chicken, parsley sauce, macaroni and potatoes, ice-cream and apple.

Mr. Mabane refused the ice and apple.

NEW JOBS FOR ITALIANS

The Government wants to employ more Italian prisoners of war in this country, and has now found a "formula" for overcoming past opposition.

There are about 400,000 Italians here already and willing to work. They have the skill and experience, and have passed the security tests.

Up to now barely 150,000 have been given jobs mostly on the land and on railways.

Many who have not yet been employed are skilled in engineering and allied trades, metals and machinery. The Government intends to place them where they will be acceptable to employers and workers, and in districts where their can be housed without local opposition.

Teachers' new pay scale accepted

The Government has accepted the Burnham Committee proposals for teachers' wage increases totalling £2,130,000.

They will come into force three years on April 1, Mr. R. A. Butler, Minister of Education, announced yesterday. Salaries will be—

Men, £300, rising by £15 a year to £525; **women,** £270, rising £12 a year to £420.

Head Teachers will get from £700-£790 (men), and from £460-£658 (women), according to size of school. There will also be additions for special qualifications.

£100,000,000 for steel plant

By BERNARD HARRIS

AT the Dorman Long meeting yesterday Lord Greenwood estimated that plans already prepared for extending and modernising our steel plants may well involve the industry in a capital expenditure of £100,000,000.

The iron and steel industry, he said, would be called on to make a great contribution to work reconstruction, but its ability to export would turn on the success in reducing production costs. Coal for example, now represented more than 2s a ton in the cost of heavy steel products, or twice as much as in 1939.

Lord Greenwood revealed that in the five years to September last the company had produced more than £500,000 tons of steel ingots, all of which had been used in the war effort.

The group had built 226 ships, helped with the construction of the Invasion harbours, and had become one of the largest producers of anthracene for fixed dyes and toluene for explosives.

Another steel company chairman to give operating details relative to war-time security but in Sir Charles War-time security but in Sir Charles Wright in his last report of Richard as a manufacturing concern.

Diversion of the works to war purposes combined with labour and coal shortages substantially reduced the company's size, and increased output. But there were increases in electrical, sheets and stampings and aluminium sheets.

In the five years 1940-44 Baldwins turnover was about £40,000,000, or £37,000,000 more on materials, £11,000,000 in wages and salaries,

and £1,800,000 in taxation. Net dividends amounted only to £500,000.

In the report of British Mechanical Productions, who are associated with Philco Radio, Brig.-General Luggs foreshadows an early increase of capital, the aim of a general scheme of refinancing of the Philco group. Profits are about £4,000 up at £395,580, out of which 10% is being paid in dividends.

Bank of England—Half-year's profits £461,403 (£437,150 for first half 1945-46) at 9 months.

Broom and Wade.—Provisional consent has been obtained for issue of £2 pay 6s. Ordinary shares at 18s 6d for each 10s held.

HOW SHARES MOVED

(share price listings)

FIREWATCHING: THE END

Britain's last 500,000 fire-watchers—in the City of London, and elsewhere in south and east England—stand down at midday tomorrow.

Mr. Herbert Morrison, Home Secretary, making the announcement in the House of Commons yesterday said:

"I should like to acknowledge the debt we owe the Fire Guards. Should attacks make it necessary I am sure they will again resume duty if called upon."

Those who have done roofspotting as their share of fire-watching are included in the relaxation of the Order, according to a Home Security official.

Budget on April 24 may be 'as you were'

Budget Day is to be April 24 it was announced in the Commons yesterday. M.P.s were guessing last night that it would be an "as-you-were" Budget, with no sensational cuts in taxes and no additions, writes the Express Political Correspondent.

290,000 have got new identity cards

During the last 12 months 290,000 applications have been made in England and Wales for the replacement of lost or destroyed identity cards, Mr. Willink, Minister of Health, said in the Commons.

That, he said, included those destroyed by enemy action.

Gough case inquiry

An "independent person"—probably a judge—is to make a public inquiry into aspects of the Gough case, Mr. Herbert Morrison, the Home Secretary, announced in the Commons yesterday.

Bull kills child

Mair Jones, 10-year-old daughter of a Rhosian, Criccieth farmer, was killed by one of her father's bulls yesterday while playing in a field.

A MINISTER

Express Staff Reporter

MR. GEORGE TOMLINSON, Parliamentary Secretary to the Ministry of Labour, and Socialist M.P. for Farnworth, Lancs, was rebuked by the Bolton county magistrates yesterday.

They were considering the case of a 36-year-old ganger, Benjamin Grime, Wild, who was accused of not complying with the Ministry's direction to work as a navvy with a Farnworth firm.

Mr. A. Lawson, for Wild, said Mr. Tomlinson wrote him a note last Sunday saying that a man should not be directed to a job below his grade or to one not under the Essential Work Order and not carrying guaranteed wages.

The National Service Officer, Mr. D. Sharrocks, said: "I have the power to direct whether it is under the Essential Work Order or not and that statement is not authentic."

Mr. Lawson: "Would you think the Parliamentary Secretary to the Ministry of Labour would know what he is talking about if he expresses an opinion."

Mr. Sharrocks: "Yes, but I would not say he was definitely conversant with the finer points of the regulations."

The magistrates' clerk, Mr. G. E. Scott, said: "If his department has ordered a prosecution against a man and he is satisfied it is irregular, one would have thought Mr. Tomlinson would have communicated with Mr. Sharrocks or the prosecuting solicitor."

Mr. Lawson said that Mr. Tomlinson was right the prosecution must fail.

Wild's direction would mean that he would get £3 16s. a week, which was liable to reductions through being rained-off. As a ganger he had been earning £6, and navvying was not under the Essential Work Order.

GO ANYWHERE

Wild told the magistrates that he was not prepared to obey the direction as it would imperial his three children. He would go anywhere if his wages were not dropped.

The chairman, Mr. W. A. Spofforth, fining him £5 and ordering him to pay £3 3s. advocate's fee, said it was improper for Mr. Tomlinson to have made any intrusion before the case came before the court.

An idea powerful enough to rebuild the world

PEOPLE MATTER has been our theme. If we believe it sincerely we shall be different persons. Our problems will be solved as we hold to this, the true basis of family and community life. . . .

If we make PEOPLE MATTER our aim, we shall have justice — we shall insist on it. But man's justice falls short of God's justice, which is fulfilled in love — God's love. For man's justice often denies love, but God's does not. Justice should be the soil in which Christian love can grow.

People cannot really matter, without love — without God. If we allow ourselves to be guided merely by man's sense of justice, there are some people we cannot like or approve. But if we would be children of God, all people will matter to us. Because they matter to God, they matter to us. *From a "Lift up your hearts" broadcast.*

PEOPLE MATTER

THE CHURCH OF ENGLAND

The Church House, Westminster, S.W.1

be a matter for prayer and careful consideration from all points of view. In such consideration, account would naturally be taken of the truth that the necessary financial support is never lacking where spiritual advance is being made.

What it might effect.

271   The method of Christian education by advertising falls into the preliminary stage of evangelism. It aims at arousing the sense of need, in order that the Gospel may be heard and accepted as the satisfaction of the need.

We do not argue that evangelism by advertising will effect conversions; though the astonishing way in which the old fashioned tract was often used of God, shows that this is by no means an impossibility. We do believe, however, that evangelism by advertising may prove of incalculable value in the preliminary stage of preparing the soil for the reception of the seed.[9]

The method of advertising can, also, integrate all other forms of evangelism; can infuse new life and vision into established forms; and can bring into touch with the Church unknown thousands now thirsting for spiritual strength and peace at heart.

Fishers of men.

272   The Church of England is the expected leader if the Church in general is to launch out in this and similar great ventures of evangelism on a national scale. But the necessary resources of artistic and professional ability, of money and influence, are distributed throughout all the denominations. While, therefore, it is the responsibility of the Church of England to take the initiative in casting wide the Gospel net, it must beckon to its partners in the other boat in order to carry through so great an enterprise.

[9] The experiment of Newspaper Evangelism and the use of advertising by the Church have already proved fruitful in Japan. See **W. H. Murray Walton**, *The Press and the Gospel.* S.C.M., 1932.

CHAPTER VI

THE CHURCH, CHRIST'S WEAPON FOR EVANGELISM

"Remember, the supreme wonder of the history of the Christian Church is that always in moments when it has seemed most dead, out of its own body there has sprung up new life; so that in age after age it has renewed itself, and age after age by its renewal has carried the world forward into new stages of progress, as it will do for us in our day, if only we give ourselves in devotion to its Lord and take our place in its service." WILLIAM TEMPLE.

Ultimately, the evidence for the credibility of the Gospel in the eyes of the world will rest upon the evidence of a quality of life manifested in the Church which the world cannot find elsewhere.[1]

The Christian's life, the acid test.

THESE words from the second chapter of our Report embody a demand which the Church can neither evade nor resent.

The Church claims that the work of redemption has delivered mankind from the slavery of sin, and has opened the Kingdom of Heaven to all believers. The reign of the Kingdom does not lie wholly in the future. It is the rule of God, introducing a system of right relationships into which the believer enters here and now; even though in this life these can never be enjoyed in all their fulness.

The world is entitled to demand that, if it is asked to accept the Christian claims, it shall be given evidence of their truth. The world looks, therefore, for some manifestation, among believers, of that higher quality of life which, as they assert, results from living in such right relationships. " By their fruits ye shall know them."[2]

274   It does not follow, however, that this new quality of life is one that the world will at once recognise as superior to its own. Not infrequently Christian standards have been regarded by some

The demand for fellowship.

1 See par. 75.
2 Matt. vii. 20

as inferior to those of the world.   Christian morality, for example, has been stigmatised as a slave morality. And Swinburne's reproach : "Thou hast conquered, O pale Galilean; the world has grown grey from Thy breath,"[3] is the classic expression of the truth that there must always be something about the Christian life which will offend rather than attract unregenerate human nature.

Nevertheless, as far as this country is concerned, the generality of men admire and desire some, at least, of those qualities which are most truly characteristic of the Christian life.   Especially do they long for fellowship.   The Christian life is one which can only be realised in fellowship, and (if it is true to itself) must be productive of fellowship.   To live in right relationship with God and with one another is to establish the very quintessence of fellowship. Unless, therefore, fellowship is plainly visible as the characteristic mark of the Church, something is radically wrong with its spiritual life, and must be remedied before the Church can discharge its calling of faithful witness to Christ, its Lord and Head.

THE FELLOWSHIP OF THE CHURCH

Fellowship, the mark of the Church.   CAN we point to fellowship as the characteristic mark of the Christian Church to-day?   Few would dare to do so, as far as the Church in this land is concerned.   To deny that true fellowship can be found within its society would indeed be foolish.   " In spite of its failure and imperfections the Church is still the greatest unifying fellowship in this world."[4]   Yet such fellowship cannot be regarded as the characteristic mark of the ordinary congregation. Clearly, there is something lacking in the spiritual life of the Church; and it must be recovered if the measures we have advocated in this Report are not to be still-born.   In other words : —

> **For effective evangelism there is need not only to recover the apostolate of the whole Church, but also the fellowship of the Church.**

3 Hymn to Proserpine.

4 Dr. William Temple, in an address to the Central Youth Council at Swanick, 1938.

The Nature of Christian Fellowship

276   The word "fellowship" is common to the vocabulary of Christian and non-Christian alike.   In the mouth of the latter it has a wide connotation, ranging from mere "mateyness" cemented, it may be, over a pint of beer, to a deep sense of community springing from the sharing in a common experience, or devotion to a common purpose.   The distinctive feature of Christian fellowship is that it alone places no limits upon its brotherhood. *Secular and Christian fellowships.*

The common Christian experience is that of sharing in the salvation wrought for *all mankind* by our Lord Jesus Christ.

The common purpose which at once inspires and fosters Christian fellowship is the furtherance of God's will in the *world*, and more particularly to "preach the Gospel to the *whole creation*."[5]

277   The Fellowship of the Church was brought into existence by the outpouring of the Holy Spirit on the day of Pentecost, uniting those who received Him in their common experience, and sealing them for their common purpose.   Indeed, the conscious fact of their possession by the One Spirit, brought to the first generation of Christians so new and overpowering an experience of fellowship, that they coined a special phrase for it, and called it *"the* Koinonia," *"the* Fellowship." *The Fellowship of the Holy Ghost.*

Pentecost thus manifested three distinctive characteristics of the fellowship of the Church.

278   *Christian fellowship is not based on human conditions.*   It does not depend upon any natural community of opinion nor of temperament.   Human fellowship derives its quality from identity of outlook or of craft.   Such accidental identity is never enough by itself to produce fellowship.   It may, as easily, produce jealousy. Moreover, accidental identity, though providing a foundation upon which fellowship can be built, yet sets a limit to its extent. *1. The basis of Christian fellowship.*

The Fellowship of the Church is neither based upon, nor limited by, any human accident.   It emerges wholly out of a supernatural experience and devotion.   Its foundation is what God has done for His people.   Its limits are what God will have His people to do.   Because it embraces all service of God, it has a place within its circle for all that is good and true in human fellowships.   But it is harder of achievement, demanding real spiritual effort.

5 Mark xvi. 15.

For this reason church people are tempted to be content with party fellowships, based upon limited community of outlook. The true fellowship of the Spirit overleaps all such considerations. It transcends the barriers of race or class, of culture or tradition: in Christ "there can be neither Jew nor Greek; there can be neither bond nor free."[6]   The Fellowship of the Church is well illustrated by Dr. Albert Schweitzer's words: "Missionaries do not regard themselves as English, Dutch or German; they are Christians who happen to be of English, Dutch or German extraction."

2. The means towards Christian fellowship.

279   Christian fellowship is not to be achieved by human means. Since Christian fellowship is supernatural, God-given, centred in a common experience of Christ and a common devotion to Christ, it is not to be attained simply by the process of coming together. Social gatherings of church people have their own value and their place in the Church's economy. But it is a delusion to suppose that they will automatically produce the fellowship of the Spirit. They give opportunity for forming human friendships. These, in turn, may be transformed into true Christian fellowship, if they are dedicated to the service of God. But not otherwise.

3. The purpose of Christian fellowship.

280   Christian fellowship is integral to the Gospel. The Fellowship of the Church is no mere adornment of, nor help towards, the Christian life. Apart from the Fellowship of the Church the promises of the Gospel cannot find complete fulfilment. In St. Paul's description of the " fruit of the Spirit " he lists nine qualities, none of which can be fully realised in isolation.[7]

On the other hand, the existence of fellowship among Christians is itself evidence that those who experience it are indeed sharing the new life of the Spirit: "We know that we have passed out of death into life, *because we love the brethren.*"[8]   So it was that when the Gospel was first proclaimed, the fellowship of the Church was also proclaimed as an essential element of God's good news: " They then that received His word were baptised . . . And they continued stedfastly in the apostles' teaching and [the] fellowship, in the breaking of bread and the prayers."[9]   To have claimed to be able to live the Christian life apart from the Christian community

6 Gal. iii. 28.
7 Gal. v. 22, 23.
8 I John: iii. 14.
9 Acts ii. 41, 42.

would have passed the comprehension of the Church of the New Testament.[10]

281   To sum up, it is clear that "the Church is not an association of men gathered together by an act of their own wills, but is a creation of God in Christ, through which, as His Body, Christ carries on His work for men . . . The first and, if fully understood, the whole duty of the Church, is truly to be the Church, the community of the Holy Spirit drawing men and nations into itself that they may become sharers in its God-given life and so fulfil their several destinies according to His purpose."[11] *The Church is fellowship.*

THE RECOVERY OF THE FELLOWSHIP OF THE CHURCH

282   It must sorrowfully be admitted that the mass of men to-day see the Church neither as a supernatural fact, nor as a necessity of the Gospel. Its fellowship is obscured by our unhappy divisions, by the lack of charity found in particular congregations, and by the absence in so many Christians of any burning desire to make Christian principles apply to ordinary life. Consequently, many who look to Christianity to provide a solution for their problems, tend to regard it as an ethical system from which they take just so much as will suit their purpose. *The situation to-day.*

No one would deny that there is a real hunger for fellowship stirring in men's hearts. The tragedy is that the fellowship of the Christian Church seems to offer them less in the way of community than is to be found in membership of a political party, or trade union, or some other secular association. The result is a loss both to those who seek fellowship outside the Church, and to the Church itself. Those outside lack what the Church alone can give through the eternal Gospel. The Church lacks the forceful contribution of those who passionately desire community of spirit and the more just ordering of society.

283   We have said that the fellowship of the Church is God-given, and cannot be achieved by human effort alone. This does not mean that there is nothing to be done from man's side. It does mean that what has to be done will not take the form of stunts; but will involve an examination of ourselves to discover where we have *The way of recovery.*

---

10 Cf. John Wesley: "Christianity is essentially a social religion; to turn it into a solitary religion is indeed to destroy it" (Works: 1872 ed., vol. v, p. 296. And again: "The Gospel of Christ knows no religion, but *social* religion, no holiness but *social* holiness" (Preface to *Methodist Hymn Book*).
11 Malvern Conference Report: Section II. A (2) and (3).

departed from God's plan, and so obstructed the full working of the Holy Spirit in the Church.

Fellowship in the Gospel.   284   As we have seen, all true fellowship is born out of the sharing in a common experience, and devotion to a common cause.   Is this true of the majority of the members of the Church to-day?   Are they bound together by the common experience of Salvation?   Do they see themselves as men and women devoted to the extension of Christ's Kingdom?   Could the average layman give a clear explanation of God's plan of salvation, or a plain answer to the question: "What is the cause to which you, as a Christian, are pledged?"   Do church people realise that the Fellowship of the Church is impossible apart from "fellowship in the Gospel"—that is, participation in the promises of the Gospel[12] and also co-operation in the furtherance of the Gospel?[13]

The fellowship of the Church militant.   285   During the war there have been many in the Forces who have found a new sense of fellowship because they knew themselves devoted to a common purpose in which the success or failure of any individual was of immense concern to all.   In that fellowship they found a new sense of purpose and dignity. To quote an army chaplain: "The soldier finds himself with a very clear purpose, that of winning the war in the military sphere.   He also finds himself part of a plan of campaign.   His own job may be a very dull one, but even so he can see that it is a necessary part of the general plan, and that is all that most of us want to know.   What gives a sense of frustration is being told to do something which seems to have no purpose.   In spite of the need for secrecy, General Montgomery gave orders before the battle of El Alamein that the plan of campaign was to be explained to all the troops.   He knew that it would make all the difference—and it did."

Such devotion the Holy Spirit of God can claim and transform within the Church into a fellowship even more intense in quality, if only its members can realise that they are pledged to fulfil a purpose—a purpose that is nothing less than the redemption of the whole world.

The requirements for Christian fellowship.   286   If, then, "all who profess and call themselves Christians" are to find themselves caught up in a fellowship of those who have accepted Christ Jesus as Saviour and serve Him as King, they need to acquire a better understanding of the Christian faith and calling,

12 I Cor: ix, 23, and Eph. iii, 6.
13 Phil. i, 5.

and also to devote their wills and lives to the sovereignty of the living God thus revealed.[14]

Teaching can present the substance of "the whole counsel of God," but it will remain a dead thing until the man by the surrender of the whole self lays himself open to receive the life and power of the Holy Spirit. Such self-oblation is the primary meaning of worship, which is also its continual expression. We pass on, therefore, to consider these two requirements for the building up of the Fellowship of the Church: the training of the Church in the faith, and the worship of the Christian Church.

THE TRAINING OF THE CHURCH IN THE FAITH

THE training of the laity in the faith has always been a chief **Ignorance** concern of faithful priests, who have toiled patiently at the task. **of the** Yet the fact remains, not only that the majority of those outside **Faith.** the Church's fellowship are extraordinarily ignorant of the Christian faith, but (and more serious) that many within the Church share their ignorance to an extraordinary degree. What is the reason for the comparative failure of persistent effort so to teach the faith that Christians may know themselves as brothers in their personal allegiance to Christ and as comrades in a great adventure of service for the carrying out of God's purpose?

Part of the explanation (as we believe) is the changed outlook and mental frame of our generation, which accounts for much of the teaching given not being assimilated. But that is only part of the answer. We must look further if we are not only to diagnose what is wrong, but make positive suggestions to meet an urgent situation.

---

14 A question is here raised which ought seriously to be faced, namely, whether this end can be fully obtained under existing conditions, whereby infant baptism is administered without any guarantee that those thus admitted to Christian membership will receive training in the Christian life and faith. We believe that we are not going beyond our terms of reference when we respectfully suggest that the Commission which has already reported on the Baptismal Office, should be followed by another to study the doctrine of the Sacrament, and in particular to consider whether the requirements necessary for the reception of its grace are, in fact, being complied with to-day.

PREACHING THE FAITH

**The impor-
tance of
preaching.**

288   There are two methods of oral teaching, both of which are required for a better understanding of the faith. There is the sermonic or lecture method, and there is the method of discussion. Though both have been employed, it is the former upon which the clergy have mainly relied. The sermon has been the chief, and often the only, teaching method, at all events for adults. The peculiar opportunities offered by the method of discussion have thus been neglected, and thereby preaching itself has been adversely affected.

In the sermon the preacher speaks with authority in the Name of the Lord. His subject should be on a level commensurate with the dignity of his commission to proclaim the "magnalia Christi"— the great things of Christ. To fulfil this high purpose, courses of sermons might be more frequent. But when the sermon is his only medium of communication with his congregation, it is almost inevitable that it should be used for other and lesser topics. The result upon the hearer is often disastrous. The irritating and repelling effect upon worshippers when the Sunday sermon is devoted to the explanation of some minor detail of Church order or ceremonial, still worse the setting forth of the preacher's personal views upon some highly controversial topic of the moment, cannot be over-estimated.

**"The com-
mon people
heard Him
gladly."**

289   In preaching there is, also, the opposite danger of expounding Christian doctrine in a manner so academic and abstracted from life, that it seems to be irrelevant to the everyday lives of the congregation.

Chaplains to the Forces know how constantly officers and men who were practising Christians, have made the appeal: "Don't preach doctrine to us, preach life." Put like this the request seems nonsense. But its meaning is as plain as its reminder is salutary: "Don't preach doctrine abstracted from life, but show us its bearing upon life." To do so with power makes great demands on the preacher—demands which are primarily spiritual rather than intellectual. He must have personal experience of the power of the Gospel which he proclaims. But the question of technique is also involved. We are told that if a religious broadcaster began his address with "To-day, as you all know, is Septuagesima", 50,000 sets would immediately be switched off. Many clergy would do well to study the manner of presentation adopted by the best religious broadcasters.

290   One great safeguard against the pitfall whether of trivial or **Bible preaching.** of academic preaching, is to return to Bible preaching. By reason of the appalling ignorance of the Bible now prevailing, it is no longer possible for the preacher to assume that even the best known Bible stories are familiar to his audience. He can no longer use the Bible as a store of illustrations.

But Bible preaching is infinitely more than making Scriptural allusions. It is the unfolding of the great themes of the Bible, and their application to the lives of men. It is the proclamation of the great verities of our religion, direct from its title deeds. Such preaching can never become trivial. Nor will it be " in the air." For it is the very genius of the Bible that it is the record of God's self-disclosure, given to men through men, and culminating in the perfect revelation of Himself through One Who was God in Man, the Eternal and Living Word.

291   Such Bible preaching cannot fail to convey a sense of the **Bible preaching universal in scope,** *universal scope* of the Gospel. For example, it is not possible to expound the teaching of the Old Testament prophets without show- ing that the will of God cannot find full expression in a morality which is merely individual, but must inevitably permeate the domains of social, industrial and political life. Furthermore, in so far as it is faithful to Bible teaching, Bible preaching will be found in sharp and definite contrast to the humanistic approach to the problems of society.

292   Neither must Bible preaching fail to emphasize the *uncom-* **and uncompromising in its demand.** *promising nature* of the Gospel. If the Church is to be a true fellow- ship of witness, it is essential that the preaching of its clergy shall be ever charged with this truth. For the function of the preacher is to confront man in the whole of his life with the living God (the God revealed in Jesus Christ) and with the whole of His claim.

TEACHING THE FAITH

293   It is obvious that the effect of such Bible preaching will often **The importance of Christian teaching.** be to raise questions in men's minds rather than to allay them. It must, therefore, be supplemented by other opportunities and other methods for training in the faith. These must increasingly be recognised as no less a normal part of the Church's armoury than the Sunday Sermon. We are not here thinking of the vital matter of the Christian teaching of children, both in our national education and in Sunday Schools or their equivalent. This has always been

the special concern of the Church. It is the new and pressing problem of the Christian teaching of adults that now concerns us.

We would urge that continuation classes after Confirmation are often even more important than preparation before Confirmation; and that systematic courses of instruction on the Christian faith and life would be greatly welcomed by numbers of habitual Church worshippers.

A new Church Catechism.
294   We have, also, one important and practical recommendation to make. A new Church catechism is required, put forth by authority, which would be fuller and more explicit than the one in the Prayer Book. This is not to decry the present Catechism. It is quite admirable as a syllabus of religious teaching. Its five parts: Church membership, the Christian faith, the Christian ethic, Worship, the Sacraments, cover the whole of life in Christ; though an amended order might be an improvement. But it requires elaboration. Its general statements need expansion, with more detailed explanation and more precise teaching. Such an expanded catechism should be the possession of every member of the Church, and form the basis of Christian education all through life. We recommend that a committee of theological scholars and teachers be appointed to give the Church a manual in catechetical form, of Christian doctrine and behaviour.[15]

Discussion groups.
295   *The Discussion Group* stands high among additional opportunities for training in the faith. It is complementary to the sermonic or lecture method. Properly conducted it is Socratic in its operation, and its efficiency may be judged by the degree in which the talking is done, not by the leader but by all the members of the group. Its aim is to encourage thinking, rather than to impart information. By this method, though information is imparted more slowly, it is more truly assimilated, by those taking part, than by listening to a discourse. It also calls for more skill and preparation from the leader than is demanded of a lecturer; and it requires training such as we have envisaged elsewhere.[16]

Study circles.
296   *Study Circles* form the main theme of the important report, *The Church and Adult Education*, published by the Central Council for Religious Education, under the chairmanship of Sir Richard Livingstone. It finds the cause of the present ignorance of the

15 Experiments in this direction have already been made: notably, *A Supplementary Instruction* on the Catechism, issued for experimental use by the Lower House of York Convention, and the Bishop of Chelmsford's *A Catechism of the Creed* (S.P.C.K. 1d.).
16 See par. 104.

fundamentals of Christianity in the fact that, "for the vast majority, religious education stops short at the point where religious interest is developing," namely, when school-leaving age is reached. "The only way to solve the problem," says Sir Richard, "is through a system of adult religious education, which will fortify the faith and deepen the religious knowledge of the believer, and will give those who have either rejected or drifted away from, or never known Christianity, the chance of learning its meaning and claim. Such a system the Church does not possess."

297   Here we are concerned with the building up in the faith of **The method** those who are already within the Church. The Report outlines a **employed.** thorough-going scheme of religious education for adults with organisers, study groups in every parish, the training of leaders, and the strengthening of such organisations as we already possess, for example, the Church of England Tutorial Classes [17] and St. Christopher's College. It also presses for co-operation between the Church and secular educational bodies, such as the W.E.A. and the L.E.A. The method suggested is "that of discussion by a group engaged in co-operative study; the teacher must be a leader rather than instructor."

298   A word of warning must, however, be sounded. It is well **The need of** to have some definite and concrete objective in view such, indeed, **an objec-** as training for evangelism will give. Just as there is the danger of **tive.** discussion groups losing themselves in the sands of sterile argument, instead of leading on to definite study; so there is the danger of study circles going round in circles.

299   *Christian Cells* belong to another and quite distinct move- **Christian** ment, which has already proved of real value for training in the **cells.** Christian life and faith. It seems to have sprung up spontaneously in many different Church quarters, and to exhibit the marks of a direct moving of the Holy Spirit. While, therefore, such cells cannot be organised or produced to order, their emergence can be regarded only with hope and expectancy. The clergy, in particular, should be eager to offer any assistance and guidance that may be asked of them. But they must be ready to give it without instrusiveness or a desire to control; with the respect that is due to a movement of the Spirit of God; and with the sympathy owed to those who are seeking painfully to discern God's will for them.

[17] 69 Great Peter Street, S.W.1.

There is already in existence an Advisory Group for Christian Cells[18] from whom full information can be obtained. We would express our conviction that the method of the cell will be found valuable in every phrase of the witness which is to lead to the reconversion of England, and that such an Advisory Group for Christian Cells should form part of the organization of the central Council for Evangelism which we recommend.

The full co-operation of the laity. 300   In view of the steady increase in the number and variety of religious activities in a parish, especially as it coincides with an acute clergy shortage, the parish priest must no longer expect, or be expected, to give detailed supervision to them all. Instead, both as regards preaching the Gospel and teaching the faith, he must cultivate an entirely new attitude towards the full co-operation of the laity in spiritual ministrations. He must be prepared to trust the laity, to delegate responsibility to them, and to encourage their initiative, reserving to himself a more general oversight, and giving himself time for spiritual leadership.

There is no reason why the conduct of informal discussion groups, and the like, should fall entirely on the clergy. In most parishes there are laymen and women well qualified for the work, especially in the ranks of the teaching profession. These should be induced to attend the leadership courses we have recommended.[19]

Already parish priests recognise that one of their most important duties is to find and train Sunday School superintendents and teachers. Group leaders should be regarded as an equally normal and important part of the parochial forces. No doubt the clergy will often find themselves members of such groups. In this case they should be careful to exercise self-restraint, and seek to stimulate rather than to dominate the discussion. But every endeavour must be made to overcome the idea that a group cannot function without the help of the parish priest, or that its importance is minimised if he is absent.

Study leads to action. 301   Study should, to be healthy, result in action. Groups for the study of the Christian faith should develop into groups to put the principles of the faith into operation. Such common action will take two forms—evangelistic and social. There will be the evangelistic presentation of the faith to individuals; and there will be the social application of the faith to the contemporary situation.

18 Townsend House, Greycoat Place, London, S.W.1, and see pars. 122 and 149-155.
19 See par. 125.

The two are bound to operate together, even as in the earthly ministry of Christ Himself. The evangelist must long to see removed all those conditions which make it difficult to know God or to live as His children. The Christian Social reformer must recognise that amid all his concern for social betterment and economic change, the centre of the problem is in human nature itself.

302   The twofold duty before the Church has been well put by **The Church's two-fold duty.** the Tambaram Conference in 1938:—" It is not enough to say that if we change the individual we will of necessity change the social order. This is a half truth, for the social order is not entirely made up of individuals now living. It is made up of inherited attitudes which have come down from generation to generation through customs, laws, institutions, and these exist in large measure independently of individuals now living. Change these individuals and you do not of necessity change the social order unless you organise these changed individuals into collective action . . . While it is a half truth to say that changed individuals will necessarily change the social order, it is also a half truth to say that social change will necessarily produce individual change. We cannot sustain a new social order or bring it into being without new men, for in the ultimate analysis the whole outer structure of society rests upon human character."[20]

303   The awakening of the social conscience of the Church has **"Church work"** enormously extended the conception of what is meant by church work. Church work can no longer be confined to that service which is peculiarly associated with a church building or parish organization. It covers every department of human life. Nothing that concerns the individual, social, political or economic welfare of the community, is outside the scope of Christian action. It is a Christian responsibility to claim each and all of the varied departments of life for God, and so to order them that they may minister according to His will and reflect His glory.

304   As all these wide and varied fields are more directly affected **Unity in diversity.** by those actually engaged in them, a form of specialization has inevitably developed in Christian action. The Church, therefore, by its very nature, must be the common meeting ground for men and women of widely differing interests, vocations, and political opinions.

20 *The World Mission of the Church* (Tambaram, 1938), p. 127.

The Church should welcome the enrichment of its life by such comprehensive diversity within its fellowship. The Church should feel its responsiblitiy to strengthen and encourage those so often called to do church work in a secular environment. The Church, too, will provide the integration of such diversity in the common offering of its members' differing activities to the service of the one God and Father of us all. In other words, Christian worship is the common element that gives unity to Christians' diverse works.

The Worship of the Christian Church

Christian worship.

AS we have stated, fellowship is the outcome of sharing in a common experience and of devotion to a common cause. In the case of the fellowship of the Church, the experience which Christians share is their common salvation, and the cause to which they are devoted is God's purpose of redemption for the world. In true worship the experience and the purpose meet and become articulated. Moreover, in worship, in the offering of life and work to God and His acceptance of them, the Holy Spirit descends upon our dead endeavour and takes it up to form a living part of the Divine activity.

The Nature of Christian Worship

Worship and holiness.

306   Christian fellowship is a call to holiness; Christian worship is an offering to a Holy God. Unless the worshipper is confronted by the vision of holiness, church worship will always be in danger of slipping into that formalism which the prophets of the Old Testament condemned, and our Lord denounced even more searchingly. The Englishman's habit of identifying religion with ethics is to be deplored, because his ethics are so often divorced from communion with the Holy God. Christian fellowship can only be experienced in its fulness when the members of the Church surrender their minds to God that he may inform their thinking, their hearts that He may infuse them with His love, and their wills that He may operate in and through them.

307   Unless their own imperfection is continually confronted by **Worship**
the vision which true worship brings of the holiness of God, not only **and**
will church people fail to experience the sense of fellowship, but **ethics.**
the actual ground of fellowship, also, will be steadily cut away
from under them. Without the continual corrective of worship, their
moral and ethical standards will tend to assimilate to the standards
of the world, lest they should be found to be clearly unattainable
in practice. A sentimental belief in a God of Love will not only fail
to arrest this process, but may also actually assist it. For instead
of proclaiming: "Be ye perfect, even as your Father who is in
heaven is perfect," it advises "Be ye good-natured, for your Father
in heaven is very good-natured."

The first duty of the Church is so to order its worship that it
unveils to men the character of God revealed in Jesus Christ: "Ye
are an elect race, a royal priesthood, a holy nation, a people for
God's own possession, that ye may show forth the excellencies of
Him who called you out of darkness into His marvellous light."[21]
This first requirement must be satisfied if the Church is to recover
its sense of fellowship, and of mutual responsibility, in the discharge
of its duty to worship and witness. Only then will the demands of
God, both upon the individual and no less upon the congregation
corporately, be seen to involve a quality of life radically at variance
with the easy going ethics of secular society, or with the formal
religion of a pious sect.

308   Unhappily, the majority of men to-day do not see that **Worship**
worship is relevant to life. In part this is due to the failure of **and life.**
Christians to manifest in their ordinary relationships that quality of
life which worship should engender. This stumbling block can
never be entirely removed in this world. The Church is not, and
cannot be, the assembly of "the spirits of just men made perfect."
It is an assembly of men in all stages of spiritual growth.
None the less, "the failure of the Church as a whole to exhibit a life
consistent with its creed,"[22] presents a standing reproach and challenge to Christians, and provides an additional motive for pressing
on unto holiness.

The failure to appreciate the relevance of worship to life is
also due to a misconception of the true nature of worship, with a
consequent confusion of worship with cult. If man is created for
the glory of God, worship (literally, the *shaping* of the *worth*
of God) is not one activity among many. It is the direction and

21 I Pet: ii, 9.
22 *The Evangelistic Work of the Church* (1918), p. 6.

right use of all man's life and powers. His daily work whereby he wins his daily bread, his contacts with his fellowmen, his friendships, his loves, his fashioning of his home, all these provide material for worship. They *become* worship in so far as by his conduct of them they reflect or shape the worth of God .

But man, by reason of his fallen nature, tends to direct his powers not to the shaping of God's worth, but to the service of his own ends: not to the reflection of God's love for all men, but to the gaining of his own advantage over his fellows. Hence come all the great evils which obscure the love of God—strife, jealousy, war and the exploitation of man by man.

Only one life has ever been true worship all through its course, the life of Him Whose meat was to the will of Him that sent Him, and to accomplish His work.[23] Other lives become worship in so far as they are conformed to His life. For that, they must be deliberately offered to Him, and laid open to receive the infusion of His Spirit with His gifts of pardon, direction and power.

Church worship.

309   The self-offering of one's life to God cannot be consciously and continuously made throughout its course. For example, the miner's daily work does in fact shape the worth of God, by making available for the use of men those valuable minerals which are the gifts of the Creator's bounty. But the miner cannot, and ought not to, be consciously offering that work to God *all the time* that he is employed at the coal face. His mind must be concentrated on the work in hand. Otherwise it will be badly done, and may even endanger his own life and that of his mates. At such times he must be thinking, not of God but of the state of the roof and the security of his props. That is the meaning of Archbishop Temple's challenging dictum that "in order to serve God properly, there are times when we must forget Him."[24]

But just because that is so, there must be times when our life and daily work are consciously and deliberately offered to God, and so transformed into worship. *This is the true function of the worship which is offered in church.* Church worship is not an activity which stands apart from the rest of life, separated, isolated and self-contained. It is not an escape from the life of every day into some different and more rarefied spiritual air. It is the offering of the life of every day that God may fashion and direct it.

23 John iv, 34.

24 Cf. Sir Jacob Astley's prayer before the Battle of Edgehill: "O Lord! Thou knowest how busy I must be this day: if I forget Thee, do not Thou forget me."

310   Nowhere is this true character of Christian worship revealed **Holy Com-**
more clearly than in the central and highest act of Christian worship, **munion.**
the Holy Communion. There we fix our eyes upon Him Whose
whole life was a perfect act of worship of His Father. There we
make memorial of the sacrifice in which that life of worship reached
its culmination.   There on our side we offer our bread and wine
(man's work upon God's gifts, typifying our use of all that God has
given us) that this imperfect oblation may be taken up into His
perfect offering, and by Him be sanctified.   There we draw near
with faith to receive into our sinful lives the new life of Him Who
died and rose again, so that, dwelling in Him and He in us, we too
may be made a reasonable, holy and lively sacrifice to the God and
Father of all.

311   The truth that the public worship of the Church is the cor- **Sunday**
porate offering to Almighty God of the *every-day* life of the **Worship.**
worshipping community, reveals the true significance and importance
of the observance of Sunday.   The purpose of the Divine ordinance
will now be recognised.   One day in seven is to be set apart as
holy in order that the other six working-days may become worship
and reflect the worth of God. This explains why the increasing
secularisation and commercialising of Sunday has been a major
factor in the widespread drift from religion.

    We are beginning to learn by painful experience that worship
and spiritual growth require stillness, quiet and the avoidance of
excitement or hurry.   Furthermore, nothing can compensate for the
loss inflicted on those who (often to minister to the selfishness of
others) are deprived of their Sunday rest and worship.   Sunday
cannot be staggered.   Sunday quietness is unobtainable on days
when the world is working.   There can be no sharing in the uplift
of worship when the churches are empty.

    In these days, particularly, of hurry and over-strain no greater
boon could be conferred on the community than the recovery of its
quiet English Sunday, to be a Day of Worship that shall infuse the
spirit of worship into the whole of life and its every activity.   In
such recovery the members of the worshipping community must lead
the way by unswerving obedience to the obligation of public worship,
even at cost and sacrifice.   To "suffer hardship" in such a cause,
is to "do the work of an evangelist."[25]

25 II. Tim. iv. 5.

THE ORDERING OF WORSHIP

Awe in worship.

312   Because the Church is entrusted with maintaining the true nature of worship, it must be the concern of the clergy so to order corporate worship that it proclaims the Gospel. Not that they should be constantly thinking of the effect of worship on the minds of the congregation. True worship is self-forgetful. There is the danger lest the desire that worship should have a missionary value may make it self-conscious, and so fail to emphasize its God-centredness.

No ordering of worship can of itself attract men into the fellowship of worship. That must be the work of the Holy Spirit. Nevertheless we can see to it that forms and methods of worship are worthy channels for the Spirit, and endeavour so to worship in spirit and in truth that the stranger may "fall down on his face and worship God, declaring that God is among you indeed."[26]

Its evangelistic power.

313   The evangelistic power of the worship of the Church cannot be over-estimated. Here, for example, is the testimony of a Jewish girl, now a faithful member of the Church: "My first experience of the worship of the Church was at Evensong on Palm Sunday. As it was my first visit to a church, most of my time was spent looking around and about, and the thing that struck me, especially during the prayers, was the rapt attention of all present on what they were doing. All heads were bowed, and at the end of each prayer the whole body of people seemed to say 'Amen' as one man. In the quietness of the prayer time I really felt that those people had quite definitely got something that I knew nothing about. There was an atmosphere. The next time I went was to the Sung Eucharist. I didn't know anything at all about the service, but the dignified manner in which it was conducted suggested to me that the God of those people must be a very wonderful person."

Catholicity in worship.

314   The effect of true worship must also be an increased apprehension of the Divine Society. Devoutness can bring with it its own peculiar liability to perversion. That type of piety which manifests itself in a demand for ever increasing religious privileges, has the effect of turning the very worship of God into a self-centred cult. The church, or the congregation, thus infected, becomes primarily concerned with itself, under the simulacrum of the worship of God.

Spiritual worship, on the other hand, is the adoring of the Divine love which binds its participants in fellowship with the

26 I Cor: xiv, 25

Father and with His Son, Jesus Christ, in the bond of the Spirit. Thereby the sympathies of all who truly share in it will be very wide, ever seeking to become co-extensive with those of its Author. Like Him, they will seek to be afflicted in all the afflictions of His children. They will see in the social evils of their day the nails crucifying Him afresh, and will feel themselves bound to spend and be spent to the uttermost in removing from the world every-thing which offends against His law of love. They will reckon no region of life as outside the scope of their calling to make God's writ run " in earth as it is in heaven." They will come to realise that the Divine Society is not only world-wide, but that it forms a living fellowship with the saints of all ages, who beyond the veil are one in service and worship with those on earth in the Com-munion of Saints.

315   In a world where men have largely forgotten the necessity **Simplicity** of worship we must be careful that our forms of worship possess **in worship.** points of contact with the unconverted. There must always be a "numinous" character about Christian worship, but numinous is not to be confused with unintelligible. Hence the importance of conducting services reverently, audibly and with simplicity. Sim-plicity does not necessarily mean absence of ceremonial. It does mean that whatever ceremonial is used must be dignified and have point and meaning.

Those responsible for the conduct of public worship should constantly be bringing their practice under review and asking them-selves whether methods, which have long been taken for granted, are in fact aiding or impeding the true worship of the congregation. Chaplains, for example, have informed us that the most intelligent men and women in the Services frequently put to them the two following questions:—" Why do clergy intone the prayers?" and "Why is there not more opportunity for silent prayer during the services?"

316   If the stranger has much to learn about worship, it should **Uniformity** at least be possible for him to feel when he comes into a worshipping **in worship.** congregation that ere long he will be able to join in its worship, and that the worship of any particular congregation is the worship of the whole Church. This lays bare a more serious division than that occasioned by diversity in *secondary* matters of worship. The extent of the unregulated variety in the order of worship within our Church, is a barrier to evangelism and a frustration of its effects. For if the stranger feels that the services are merely the services of

a particular congregation, he not only misses the glory of worshipping within the Communion of Saints, but he also feels ill at ease when he moves to another parish.

Loyalty to the Anglican tradition,

317   We cannot escape the challenge: " Is the Church of England a mere congregationalism disguised as a Church by the fact of establishment, or has it a deep unity of character derived from its distinctive response to the Word of God?" Prayer Book revision can only tinker with the problem, if this deeper question goes unanswered. Historically the Church of England is a part of the Catholic Church which sought seriously to face the challenge of the Reformation, and to continue to stand as a Church "distinguished from all puritan and papal innovations, and adhering to the doctrine of the Cross."[27] Theologically, it can only be justified if there remains alive within it a painful and creative tension between its Catholic heritage and the permanently valid insights of the Reformation. There must always be some who tend to one of its poles, some who tend to the other. But they are held together by a loyalty which consists precisely in recognising both.

and liturgy.

318   Our liturgy and formularies were hammered out in the white heat of the original struggle and provide us, not necessarily with the final form of its solution, but with an example of the temper in which it must still be conducted. Loyalty to that ceaseless and costly act of witness, can alone regenerate in the Church of England such a conception of loyalty to ordination vows as will restrain lawlessness in the conduct of worship, and such a sense of living Churchmanship as will deliver congregations from mere partisanship.

On the Continent the persecuted churches, Roman Catholic and Protestant, have discovered a "confessional life" which sees the great issues of the sixteenth and seventeenth centuries as also being contemporary. The Church of England has a historical experience no less worth recovering. If it is to face the even deeper crisis of the twentieth century, it must know again the costly loyalty of the most decisive epoch in its history, and make it the starting point of present witness. When its clergy and laity once more show that kind of life, it will be more deeply effective in its evangelism, and will offer to its members and converts a more significant worship.

Ignorance of worship.

319   It must, however, be remembered that it is very difficult to find any contacts between the liturgical worship of the Church and

27 See Dr. G. K. A. Bell's *Brief Sketch of the Church of England.* "Thomas Ken (1637-1711), Bishop of Bath and Wells."

the minds of a generation to whom all forms of worship, however simple, are unfamiliar. Indeed, evacuation, and the experience of chaplains in the Services, have shown that vast numbers of people are ignorant even of the Lord's Prayer.

Let us grant the worst, and still affirm that it would be an almost irretrievable blunder if, during the interim period of the re-conversion of England, the traditional forms of public worship were scrapped in favour of an unrestricted medley of popular services. We should do non-worshippers an injury if we led them to suppose that worship does not require a life-long apprenticeship in the greatest of all arts. We should inflict an even greater injury on habitual worshippers if their accustomed standard of worship, evolved through centuries of adoring faith, was reduced to what was agreeable to a semi-pagan understanding. The situation undoubtedly demands painstaking sympathy, but also the wise avoidance of panic remedies.

320 Even for a "people's service" it is quite possible to retain **"People's** the liturgical framework, for example of Evening Prayer, and **Services."** make it perfectly intelligible to those unused to public worship. If the whole service is not on a specially printed sheet, restrained directions can point to the appropriate place and page in the Prayer Book.[28] Short explanations can interpret the order and parts of the worship and, more particularly, can make all the difference to the understanding of the lessons. Above all, if lessons, psalms, hymns and prayers are carefully selected round a central theme, previously announced, the service itself becomes not only worshipful but an instruction in worship.[29] We believe that, in present circumstances, such elasticity within clear limits of liturgical conformity, should be allowed and encouraged under the direction of the Bishops. The Archbishops' Liturgical Committee could render valuable and welcome help, by drawing up both in outline, and also in full, forms of simple services on these lines, to be published with authority. The real solution, however, lies with the congregation itself. For the witness of true worshippers can be a cogent missionary force which compels the avowal of the stranger within the gates that "the God of these people must be a very wonderful Person."

321 This emphasises the necessity for the better training of **Training in** congregations in worship. It is no exaggeration to say that the **worship.** average member of the Church tends to think of worship as some-

28 See Recommendation, par. 350.
29 See also par. 92.

thing done for him, his part being a passive "amen." The worshipper must learn that the prayers and praises of his lips involve their constant application to his life, and the offering of himself to do the will of God.

In this connection we recall the words of Archbishop William Temple to the Upper House of Convocation: "I think that once in about five years there should be in every church a course of sermons on the Prayer Book services, explaining their structure and why the various elements in them are arranged as they are. We often forget the value, which all teachers should remember, of frequent repetition of what is of fundamental importance, and the danger of so taking for granted what is fundamental that in the result we never teach it at all."[30]

Such teaching would enable the worshipper to commend and explain the worship of the Church to others. It would also help him to realise that it is the genius of the Church to put upon the lips of its members the prayers and praises of the saints, seeing that through the power of worship the least and humblest may become one with the saints.

THE MISSING HALF OF CHURCH-LIFE TO-DAY

The Church out of church. 322   The Fellowship of the Church is integral to the Gospel. But in the life of the ordinary parish church, though it is possible to see the People of God met for worship, where else can the Fellowship of the Church be expressed and experienced? The worshipping community of Sunday seems, during the week, to be broken up into segregated Church organizations, divided up according to age, sex, interests and the like. The question has to be faced: "Where can the Church be met and known, otherwise than when it is sitting in its pews?" "Where can old and young, rich and poor, educated and uneducated, meet in a single fellowship, because they are already members one of another in Christ?" "Where, and how, can the *worshipping* community become a working and witnessing community?"

Experiments in community. 323   There are still a few places in England where the daily life of those who worship together is a community life, of which their common worship is the offering to God. But, for the most part, the community life which Christian worship pre-supposes awaits to be engendered and built up. It will need long, patient and deliberate

---

[30] *Chronicle of Convocation*, 1942 (October), No. 3, p. 318.

experimenting to devise means whereby the unity of a congregation in Christ can be given corporate expression in daily life.

In some parishes the experiment is being tried of a Church Meeting where members of the Sunday congregation are invited to meet each other and discover their corporate responsibility; though the plan breaks down where congregations are large. There are other possible expedients; and other experiments of a different character are being attempted. The great matter is that some means should be sought whereby, in the ordinary round of parish life, that common meeting-place may be provided which is no longer (or seldom) afforded by ordinary social circumstance, and yet without which a worshipping congregation can never become a family.

324   Then, be it remembered that fellowship is never found by **Evangelism** seeking it as an end in itself. Fellowship, as we have seen, is the **the solution.** bye-product of sharing in a common purpose, and of devotion to a common cause. The way to fellowship is to combine in evangelism

towards the conversion of England.

CONCLUSION.

"Christ wrote no book; He left in the world as His witness a 'body' of men and women upon whom the Spirit came. There was to be nothing stereotyped. The living Society—The Church—was to be the primary witness."

WILLIAM TEMPLE.

325 In evangelism we are directly confronted with the cardinal **God's** **sovereign** Christian doctrine of God's sovereign grace. The doctrine acknow- **grace.** ledges that, from first to last, salvation is a downward act of intervention from God to man. It is generally recognised that the fruits of salvation—forgiveness, power and eternal life—are all the free gifts of God through Christ. They can only be accepted. They can neither be merited nor achieved by man. But there is the further truth that even the *acceptance* of salvation is not the outcome of the human will alone, but is due to the moving and prompting of the Holy Spirit, inclining us to decision. Even when we begin to seek after God, it is because the Saviour has already found us.

The doctrine of God's sovereign grace sets forth a guiding principle that must condition all evangelistic effort. It draws a clear distinction between the duty to evangelise which is incumbent on all Christians, and the response to evangelism which must be left in the hands of God.

326 We cannot predict that, at any given place or at any given **Moments of** time, a new evangelistic zeal or new evangelistic methods will pro- **Divine** **moving** duce a commensurate movement of the people back to God. Instead, the history of Christianity presents us with the phenomena of moments of Divine moving when, apart (as it seems) from human planning, and beyond human expectation, a man or a movement suddenly emerges, and a revival ensues out of all proportion to the quality of the human agency involved.

These moments of Divine moving are indicated in the Bible by such phrases as "waiting upon the Lord," God "visiting" His people,[1] the "hour" which dictated Christ's movements, "seasons of refreshing from the presence of the Lord,"[2] "opened doors."[3]

1 Luke i, 68.
2 Acts iii, 19.
3 Acts xiv, 27; I Cor: xvi, 9; II Cor: ii, 12.

All of them signify the intervention of God as exemplified at the Incarnation: "when the fullness of the time came, God sent forth His Son."[4] History, too, gives evidence of such outstanding and, humanly speaking, inexplicable moments of Divine moving, to mention only the Franciscan movement, that of the Friends of God led by John Tauler, and the Evangelical revival of John Wesley.

Moments of opportunity.

327   It is noteworthy that these days of God seem to occur at times of upheaval and change (such as our own), when men have come to the end of their resources, and thus look to the inter-position and redemption of God: for "when the heart begins to despair of human methods, and falls back again upon God, then God's help begins to work through human weakness."

On the human level, therefore, such moments of Divine mov-ing are moments of opportunity. They are times when, in the lives of men or the history of a people, individuals or communities are more disposed to open their hearts to hear and accept the Christian Gospel, and when human wills are more inclined to make the great decision and to surrender to the claims of Christ. Thus, not only must the evangelist watch for the signs of the times and be ready for moments of Divine moving, but he must also "buy up" these moments of opportunity and turn them into moments of response.

Faithful Witness.

328   The question whether any evangelistic effort will coincide with such a moment of Divine moving, and so of opportunity, is not for the evangelist to ask. "Bearing witness to the unique saving activity of God in Christ is . . . indispensably part of the saving activity itself."[5] Faithful witness is demanded of us "whether they hear or whether they will forbear."[6] The Church has its marching orders to preach the Gospel everywhere, at all times, to all the people. For the Gospel's sake we are to become all things to all men, that we may by all means save some.[7]

The attitude at all costs to be avoided is that complacency which is satisfied with a conventional setting forth of the faith inside the Church, while the great mass of the population remains out-side.

Whether or no God allows us to see the fruit of our labours, there should be in us a Christ-like heart which so cares for people

---

4 Gal. iv. 4
5 See Dr. H. H. Farmer: *The Servant of the Word*, p. 21.
6 Ezek. ii, 5.
7 I Cor: ix, 22, 23.

that we are content to go on living for them and serving them, leaving the result with God.

329   We urge that the Church should confront the task of the **Expectancy.** conversion of England with a deep sense of expectancy of what God can accomplish through human agency, but with a questioning of ourselves as His agents for evangelism.

As clergy and laity alike undertake the obligation of being a witnessing Church, there is good reason to expect "seasons of refreshing from the presence of the Lord." For, as Nicholas Berdyaev points out in his *Freedom of the Spirit*, "it is only during periods when custom and external tradition are obstinately insisted upon that religion lacks a mystical element, and men's eyes are blind to the vision of God. This is inevitably recovered during periods when tradition and custom are being subjected to catastrophic disturbances. It is then that mysticism of the type associated especially with the work of the Holy Spirit becomes dominant. A period of renewed spirituality within Christianity is bound to be one in which there will be hitherto unprecedented manifestations of the Holy Spirit."

There are, indeed, some who believe that they can already hear "the sound of marching in the tops of the mulberry trees."[8]

330   May not the possibility of revival be changed to certainty **Consecra-** if the Church with full faith consecrates itself to the task of making **tion.** the present passage from one age into another a moment of opportunity to be bought up? The answer lies with ourselves.

> "The only spiritual dynamic is the Living Spirit of the Crucified and Risen Christ Himself. The whole . . . world is awaiting the release of this vital force through human personalities, vitalised by the Holy Spirit, and witnessing with a new power to the Cross of Christ as the central fact of faith and life. We submit that the spiritual dynamic for such a compelling witness is, in the good purpose of God, always available. But there is nothing in the Bible or in the experience of the Church to suggest that it is available cheaply. Each marked release of the Holy Spirit of God in human lives must be at the cost of definite surrender and prayer."[9]

8 I Chron: xiv. 15.
9 *The Findings of the Conference of Christian Workers among Moslems* (Jerusalem, 3rd to 7th April, 1924).

APPENDICES

A. RECOMMENDATIONS AND FINDINGS

B. BIBLIOGRAPHY

APPENDIX A.

RECOMMENDATIONS AND FINDINGS

The Recommendations are in **black type.**

I. EVANGELISM. THE RESPONSIBILITY OF THE WHOLE CHURCH

Towards the Conversion of England.

331 The state of the Christian religion in this country urgently calls for definite action.

That definite action is no less than the conversion of England to the Christian faith.

World-wide evangelism is a categorical obligation, explicit in the charge given by our Lord to His Church, and is to be obeyed as such. (Par. 87.)

The Apostolate of the laity.

332 The duty of evangelism is laid upon the *whole* Church, not only upon the ordained ministry.

(1) *By every means possible the clergy must be set free from all hindrances, spiritual as well as material, which prevent them from exercising an evangelistic ministry. More particularly must they be given time to fulfil their primary responsibility of training the laity for evangelism.* (Pars. 88-106.)

(2) *Without the participation of the laity the conversion of England is impossible.* (Par. 111.)

Not only are the clergy too few in number (par. 106), but by reason of their special calling and pastoral duties they have not the opportunity of permeating every section of the community, such as is afforded to the lay-priesthood of believers. (Pars. 128-130.)

II. THE PREPARATION OF THE WHOLE CHURCH FOR EVANGELISM

333   We recommend that the Archbishops, together with the A call to
House of Bishops, call the whole Church, clergy and laity alike, to action.
review their responsibility as the Body of Christ (par. 281), and
rethink the obligation of their Ordination (par. 88) and Confirmation (par. 112) vows in terms of the Master's command to preach
the Gospel.

334   As far as we can see this would involve : —   First steps.
(1) *Gatherings for the Clergy*, for the purpose of renewing their
resources of spiritual life and power.   (Par. 90.)
(2) *Conventions for Church-people*.   (Par. 121.)   These would take
(or combine) two forms : —
       (a) Conventions for the deepening of the spiritual life.
       (b) Conventions to teach Christian faith and practice.
(3) *Schools for Evangelism* for the clergy and laity who will emerge
from such Conferences and Conventions as potential leaders in
evangelism.   (Pars 122-125.)
       We recommend that in every diocese, when Conference and
Conventions are arranged, preparation be also made for the training of leaders in evangelism.

III. EVANGELISM. PROCLAIMING THE GOSPEL

A. EVANGELISM AND THE PARISH

335   *The first, chief and essential method of evangelism is for* Parochial
every parochial ministry to be an evangelistic ministry.   (Pars. 91 Evangelism.
and 148.)
       To be effective, an evangelistic ministry cannot be exercised
by the parish priest alone, but needs the co-operation of the congregation.   (Pars. 92-95.)

336   *To this end we draw particular attention to the value of the* Christian
Cell Movement, as affording perhaps the best evangelistic agency for Cells.
our times; though this is not to decry the value of the Parochial
Mission.   (Pars. 122, 148-155, 299 and 160-176.)
       The cell, group or team method operates effectively both in
parishes, and also in factories, business-houses and the like.
(Pars. 148-155.)

Discussion Groups.

337   *Discussion Groups should, also, become a normal activity of parochial organization.*   (Pars. 104, 215, 295.)

The *Padre's Hour* has proved the success of the method of informal discussion for reaching non-worshipping members of the community.

The experience thus gained with the Forces should be placed at the disposal of the whole Church.

Bishops' Messengers.

338   *We suggest that the use of Bishop's Messengers be extended, and include laymen as well as women.*   (Par. 110.)

Bishop's Messengers would be the representatives of the Bishop, acting with his authority and under his orders, in the parishes they visit.

B. Evangelism and the Nation

A united front.

339   Evangelism on a national scale can only be attempted by presenting, as far as possible, a united front in co-operation with other Christian communions.   (Par. 75.)

We advise that, whenever possible, evangelistic campaigns in areas should take the form of parallel campaigns.   (Par. 159.)

In a parallel campaign the various churches and chapels each conduct their own mission, but as the organization is central it is also seen to be one united effort. (See Appended Note on Ecumenical Co-operation, p. 96.)

Modern Agencies of Propaganda.

340   The religious broadcasts of the B.B.C. have shown what might be accomplished if the Church employed, for the purpose of evangelism, the great cultural agencies of propaganda—the cinema, the drama, the Press and the like.   (Pars. 217-254.)

The majority of the Commission believes that the Church should make an adventure in Christian education through advertising, upon a nation-wide scale, and with expert advice in what is a highly specialised art.   (Par. 255-272.)

A Publicity Department for the Church.

341   Few questions are of greater or more pressing importance, at the present time and in existing circumstances, than the use of methods of publicity for proclaiming the Gospel.

We recommend that, as a matter of urgency, pending the carrying into effect of the organization we shall suggest, and for the avoidance of an immediate call on Assembly funds, the Press and Publications Board be requested, as a temporary measure, to set up an organization on the lines of its Press sub-committee, with a view to making effective use of special agencies of publicity.   (Par. 267.)

IV. EVANGELISM. PREPARING FOR THE GOSPEL.

342   The four chief formative influences in the building of **Formative** character are (1) the Church, (2) the Home, (3) Education, (4) the **Influences.** Economic Order of Society. Each is important in producing an environment and mental outlook conducive to the reception of the Gospel.

A. THE CHURCH.

343   The Church, by its fellowship, teaching and worship, is **The Church,** intended to be the Divine agency for evangelism, as the Body of **the Divine agency for** Christ in the world. (Par. 87.) **evangelism.**

CHURCH FELLOWSHIP

344   *The Fellowship of the Church* requires to be made more **1. The** articulate by experiments in giving congregations opportunities **Fellowship of the** of meeting together at other times than public worship, and of **Church.** uniting for the fulfilment of their corporate responsibility. (Pars. 322, 323.)

Even as fellowship is required for evangelism, so evangelism will itself prove the surest means of achieving fellowship. (Par. 324.)

CHURCH TEACHING

345   *High among the teaching agencies of the Church, we place* **2. The Teaching** *Preaching.* (Pars. 93, 215 and 288-292.) **Office of the Church,** In the training of the clergy the Ministry of the Word must **Preaching.** receive an attention commensurate with the position it occupies in the Ordinal. (Par. 102.)

346   *A system of Adult Religious Education, throughout the* **Adult Religious** *Church and Nation, needs to be built up under the leadership of the* **Education.** *Central Council for Religious Education.* (Par. 296.)

Co-operation with the B.B.C. in its efforts to disseminate Christian teaching is greatly to be desired. (Par. 233.)

The Church must, also, co-operate with the L.E.A. in providing for adult classes on religious subjects, such as find their place in the Education Act, 1944, and in seeing that Christian teaching forms part of the curriculum of County Colleges and the like. (Par. 297.)

347   We draw attention to the value of Teaching Missions both **Teaching** in equipping church-people as evangelists, and in being themselves **Missions.** proved instruments for evangelism. (Par. 161-163.)

A new Church Catechism.

348   **We recommend that a committee be appointed to draw up an expanded form of the Church Catechism, and that when compiled it should be put forth with authority.** (Par. 294.)

CHURCH WORSHIP

3. The Worship of the Church.

349   *A fresh understanding of the meaning of Worship is required* (pars. 306-311); neither can too great attention be given to the planning and conduct of Church Services. (Pars. 92 and 312-315.)

Liturgical services require explanation and elucidation if casual attenders or enquirers are to understand them. (Pars. 319, 320).

Regular worshippers, too, need periodically to be informed and reminded of the structure and purpose of the various elements that make up the Services of the Prayer Book. The sense of true worship thus engendered provides the best education in worship for the casual visitor. (Pars. 320, 321.)

Popular Services.

350   **We recommend that, for the gathering in of non-worshippers, elasticity be allowed in the conduct of the services of the Church, providing that the framework of liturgical worship is preserved. There is also urgent need for a People's Prayer Book with standardised paging.** (Pars. 316-318 and 320.)

Sunday Observance.

351   It is essential for the Worship of the Church that Sunday should be safeguarded from the inroads of secularisation and commercialism. The setting apart of one day in seven is of Divine appointment. (Par. 311.)

B.   THE HOME

The Family.

352   The Family is the unit of community, whether of Church or State. The fellowship of the Church and its worship should be built upon the principle of gathering into one the various households of faith. (Par. 131.)

Family Prayers.

353   We draw attention to the importance of making a determined effort to re-introduce the practice of Grace before meals, and of families praying together in the home. Printed cards with Graces and simple Family Prayers, for distribution to householders, would greatly assist the work of parish priests. (Par. 132.)

Bible reading.

354   The regular habit of the daily reading of the Holy Scriptures must be taught and encouraged as an essential part of the ordered Christian life, and of home religion.

We press that steps should be taken to facilitate the publication of the Bible at a moderate price in a more attractive form. (Par. 133.)

355   **We recommend that a Commission be appointed by the** Holy
Convocations to consider the doctrine of the Sacrament of Holy Baptism.
Baptism, with special reference to the requirements for Infant
Baptism, and how the Church is to meet the difficulty of the
provision of suitable sponsors.   (Par. 286, footnote.)

C. EDUCATION

356   The Central Council of Religious Education should receive National
every support and encouragement in seizing opportunities, presented Education.
by the Education Act, 1944, for Christian instruction and worship
throughout the whole national scheme of education.   (Par. 23.)

357   Seeing that education in sociology and economics is in- Schools of
creasingly required for Government appointments and for industrial Economics.
and commercial posts, the ordinary teaching in Schools of
Economics should be supplemented by lectures on the Christian
doctrine of man. (Interim Report on the *Return of Men and Women
from War Service,* Part. I, sec. 3.)

358   Scientific manuals for ordinary readers are urgently needed, Scientific
written by leading scholars who are Christians.   They would set Manuals.
forth impartially the truths of science, but their latent Christianity
would have a greater effect than specifically Christian text-books.
(Par. 249.)
D.   THE ECONOMIC ORDER

359   Evangelism and the redemption of the temporal order are The King-
inter-related means of bringing in the Kingdom of God.   (Pars. dom of
140, 215.) God.

The economic order of society, even as the natural order of
the universe, must "declare the glory of God."   (Par. 135).

It must also enable every individual to develop full personality in community, and to recognize working life as a stewardship
from God and as service to man.   (Pars. 27, 28, 301, 308.)

Social environment must not be such as to give the lie to the
principles of the Gospel when proclaimed, or to make it unneces-
sarily difficult for hearers to accept the Gospel.   (Par. 215.)

360   Church people have an evangelistic duty towards the The Church
community at large.   (Par. 303.) and the
Community.
They must act in the spirit of Christ in the existing economic
order in which they find themselves.   (Par. 137.)

They must band together to bring the Christian principles of love and justice to bear upon the ordering of their particular profession, trade or craft. (Par. 136.)

They must fit themselves for the right use of their social and political responsibilities, and be prepared to accept positions of influence in Parliament, in municipal government, on boards of management and in industrial and commercial posts. (Par. 138.)

V. ORGANIZATION

Zech. iv, 6. *361*   We recognize that evangelism can only be organised where human channels hold themselves open to God's grace.

Diocesan Machinery. *362*   Though some organization will be necessary for the diocesan discharge of the obligation to evangelise, we do not advocate any prescribed form.

Some machinery will undoubtedly be required to arrange missions, conventions, retreats, conferences, schools of different kinds, and to plan definite evangelistic advance.

There are several ways by which the missionary energy of a diocese can be released through prayer and consultation among those entrusted with evangelistic responsibility. The lead may be given by a diocesan Evangelistic Council, or by an informal body consisting of those in various diocesan organisations, or by a department of an already existing Diocesan Missionary Council.

We desire, however, to make two suggestions:—

(1) *A Diocesan Missioner or Director of Evangelistic work will be needed to initiate and carry into effect diocesan plans for evangelism.*
(2) *A Diocesan House will be needed in each diocese to be the home of its evangelistic activity.*

A Central Council for Evangelism. *363*   We realise, however, that evangelism is no departmental matter, but runs through the whole range of the Church's activity.

Some central organization will be required to implement the suggestions of this Report, and to co-ordinate evangelistic enterprise.

We recommend that the Archbishops be requested to set up a Council for Evangelism, on the lines of the Council on Foreign Relations.

Such a Council would take the place of the still existent Archbishops' Evangelistic Committee, appointed in 1934, whose good work was terminated by the war.

APPENDIX B.

BIBLIOGRAPHY

A selected list of books, representing many points of view.

CHAPTER I

THE SITUATION BEFORE THE CHURCH

The Churches survey their Task. Ed. J. H. OLDHAM. (The Report of the Conference at Oxford, July, 1937, on Church, Community and State.) Allen & Unwin. 5/-.

This volume gives full guidance on the main problems confronting the Church at the present time.

The Hope of a New World. S.C.M. 7/6. ⎱
                                        ⎰ WILLIAM TEMPLE.
The Church looks forward. S.C.M. 7/6. ⎱

These two books contain some of Dr. Temple's most forward looking pronouncements.

Citizen and Churchman. WILLIAM TEMPLE. Eyre & Spottiswoode. 3/6.

A further development of A. D. Lindsay's book *The Two Moralities*, written with all Dr. Temple's usual lucidity.

Faith in Dark Ages. F. R. BARRY. S.C.M. 2/6.

What has Christianity to say ? F. R. BARRY. S.C.M. 6/-.

Bishop Barry always writes with a clear conception of the world's challenge to the Church, and in these two books gives us good guidance on many aspects of the Church's faith and life.

The Resurrection of Christendom. J. H. OLDHAM. C.N-L. Books. Sheldon Press. 1/6.

A good introduction to the whole contemporary problem by the well-known Editor of the Christian News Letter.

Effective Religion. T. E. JESSOP, M.C. Epworth Press. 5/-.

A very interesting and incisive study of many aspects of contemporary Christianity.

Real Life is Meeting. J. H. OLDHAM AND OTHERS. C.N-L. Books. Sheldon Press. 1/6.

A small but really valuable book on current religious problems.

Secular Despair and Christian Faith. ALEC R. VIDLER. S.C.M. 2/-.

Useful from the point of view of the challenge of religion to life.

The Fate of Modern Culture. J. V. LANGMEAD CASSERLEY. Signpost Series. Dacre Press. 1/6.

A very clever diagnosis of the present situation created by modern science and civilisation.

The Church and the New Order. WILLIAM PATON. S.C.M. 6/-.

A survey of world conditions from a Christian standpoint with a view to the better ordering of peoples after the war.

Christianity and World Order. G. K. A. BELL. Penguin. 1/-.

Probably the best contemporary study of international affairs from the Christian standpoint.

Redeeming the Time. Centenary Press. 12/6. ⎫
                                                      ⎬ JACQUES MARITAIN.
The Rights of Man. Centenary Press. 5/-. ⎭

Like all Maritain's writings they are not easy to read, but they are extremely relevant, especially the latter.

The Fate of Man in the Modern World. NICHOLAS BERDYAEV. S.C.M. 1/-.

Like all Berdyaev's books, of first-rate importance in spite of its size.

Secular Illusion or Christian Realism. D. R. DAVIES. Eyre & Spottiswoode. 3/6.

Brilliant and challenging, the book exposes the fallacies underlying modern civilisation and makes clear the essential contribution which Christianity can make to the world in the future.

The Two Moralities. A. D. LINDSAY. Eyre & Spottiswoode. 3/6.

A clear account of the dilemmas confronting the Christian as he endeavours to play his part in modern life.

The Church and Politics. S. C. CARPENTER. Centenary Press. 2/6.

Another of those "great little books" which contain much wisdom and teaching in small compass.

Religion and the Rise of Capitalism. R. H. TAWNEY. Pelican. 1/-.

Probably the most comprehensive historical survey of social and economic developments since the Reformation.

Law and Love. Prof. T. E. JESSOP. S.C.M. 6/-.

A penetrating analysis of Christian ethics from one special angle, but extremely effective.

Diagnosis of Our Times. KARL MANNHEIM. Kegan Paul & Co. 10/6.

This is an extremely able book by a leading authority on the many problems connected with Democracy and Modern Civilisation.

The Christian and the World of To-morrow. BISHOP OF CHELMSFORD. Church Book Room Press. 2/6.

A useful handbook for the times.

AN AGE WITHOUT STANDARDS (page 5)

An Interpretation of Christian Ethics. REINHOLD NIEBUHR. S.C.M. 6/-.

A very able and characteristic treatment of the ethical implications of the Christian religion. A really valuable study.

Christian Behaviour. C. S. LEWIS. Centenary Press. 2/6.

A brilliant account of Christian ethical principles.

The Two Humanities. D. R. DAVIES. James Clark & Co. 7/6.

A rather trenchant and even scathing exposure of the trends implicit in modern society and the challenge presented by the Christian religion.

Education for a World Adrift. RICHARD LIVINGSTONE. C.U.P. 2/6.

A book largely concerned with the training of character from a Christian standpoint.

What is Christian Marriage ? A. T. MACMILLAN. Macmillan. 8/6.

A concise presentation of the problems presented by Christian marriage in modern circumstances.

The Threshold of Ethics. K. E. KIRK. Skeffington. 3/6.

Deals with Christian morals from modern standpoints, e.g., psychological, evolutionary, etc.

ENGLISH CHARACTER THE HERITAGE OF THE PAST (page 5)

English Social History. G. M. TREVELYAN. Longmans. 21/-.

The title describes the scope of this work.

The Free Church Tradition in the Life of England. E. A. PAYNE. S.C.M. 6/-.

A treatment of the Free Church position and the problems involved.

Religion in the Victorian Era. L. ELLIOTT-BINNS.

A very illuminating survey.

The Middle Ages (page 7)

The Medieval Village. G. G. COULTON. C.U.P. 25/-.

A brilliant and authoritative description of medieval life based on contemporary sources.

Social Life in Britain from the Conquest to the Reformation. G. G. COULTON. C.U.P. 25/-.

A survey of every aspect of medieval life, profusely illustrated from original sources.

Medieval People. EILEEN POWER. Methuen. 7/6.

A fascinating study of medieval personalities illustrating conditions of life.

English Life in the Middle Ages. L. F. SALZMAN. O.U.P. 10/6.

A concise description of practically every aspect of medieval life.

The Industrial Revolution (page 8)

Lord Shaftesbury. F. M. G. HIGHAM. S.C.M. 6/-.

The latest study of this well-known pioneer in social reform.

Christian Social Reformers of the Nineteenth Century. Various authors, edited by HUGH MARTIN. S.C.M. 3/6.

A useful series of biographical studies of outstanding social reformers of the nineteenth century.

The Present Scientific Age (page 9)

Science and the Spiritual. T. E. JESSOP. C.N-L. Books. Sheldon Press. 1/6.

A most interesting book revealing some of the limitations of science.

Biology and Christian Belief. W. O. GREENWOOD. S.C.M. 6/-.

The title describes the contents.

Secular Education (page 10)

What is Christian Education? MARJORIE REEVES and JOHN DREWETT. C.N-L. Books. Sheldon Press. 1/6.

A small but first-rate book on the subject. Much more helpful than many larger books.

CHAPTER II

THE GOSPEL

Christus Veritas. WILLIAM TEMPLE. Macmillan. 10/-.

> The theological sequel to his earlier and more philosophical *Mens Creatrix*. Essentially a powerful presentation of essential Christian truths. Reference should be made, however, to his remarks in *Thoughts in Wartime*, page 98, revealing some modification of standpoint.

Christian Doctrine. J. S. WHALE. C.U.P. 7/6.

> One of the most stimulating doctrinal treatises produced in recent years.

The Doctrine of the Trinity. LEONARD HODGSON. Nisbet. 15/-.

> A very able study of an essential Christian doctrine.

Towards Belief in God. H. H. FARMER. S.C.M. 8/6.

> A good introduction to the subject.

Broadcast Talks. C. S. LEWIS. Centenary Press. 2/6.

> One of the best books in existence for putting into the hands of the unbeliever.

The Ground of Faith. OLIVER QUICK. Nisbet. 5/-.

> A very careful examination of contemporary unbelief with suggestions for combating it.

Christian Beliefs and Modern Questions. OLIVER QUICK. S.C.M. 1/6.

> A small but very valuable book on essential Christian doctrines.

The Faith and Modern Thought. WILLIAM TEMPLE. Macmillan. 3/-.

> A good introduction to Christian theology though written as long ago as 1919. Contains much that is permanently valuable.

History and the Gospel. C. H. DODD. Nisbet. 6/-.

> A very able study of Christianity as a historical religion. Rather difficult to summarise, but contains a valuable survey of the Gospel and modern criticism vindicating the historical element in Christianity.

The Apostolic Preaching and its Development. C. H. DODD. Hodder and Stoughton. 5/-.

> This book established the importance of the distinction between the apostolic preaching of the Gospel and the apostolic teaching of Christian moral principles.

The Holy Spirit and the Church. F. A. COCKIN. S.C.M. 2/6.

> A very good introduction to the doctrine of the Holy Spirit.

The Authority of the Faith. Various authors. Vol. I., Tambaram Reports. O.U.P.

> A particularly useful volume on modern theological problems.

M

Christ in the Gospels. A. E. J. RAWLINSON. O.U.P. 6/6.

A very satisfying interpretation of the Christology of the Gospels.

The Christian Message in a non-Christian World. H. KRAEMER. Edinburgh House Press. 8/6.

Described by Dr. Temple as "likely to remain for many years to come the classical treatment of its theme." Invaluable as a preparation for any form of Evangelistic or Missionary activity.

THE PRESENTATION OF THE GOSPEL (page 24)

The Divine-Human Encounter. EMIL BRUNNER. S.C.M. 8/6.

The latest work by this well-known author of Biblical doctrine and the Christian revelation.

Christian Faith and Life. WILLIAM TEMPLE. 3/-. S.C.M.

Lectures originally delivered in Oxford to undergraduates; extremely relevant and helpful.

THE NATURE OF GOD (page 25)

God in Christian Thought and Experience. DEAN MATTHEWS. Nisbet. 12/6.

A case in which the title of the work really does explain the contents. God's redemptive intervention in human history.

The World and God. H. H. FARMER. Nisbet. 12/6.

Deals with miracles and prayer in relationship with the over-ruling providence of God.

THE MEANING OF SIN (page 25)

The Mastery of Evil. R. LLOYD. Centenary Press. 3/6.

A brilliant exposure of the seriousness of evil.

Down Peacocks Feathers. D. R. DAVIES. Centenary Press. 5/-.

A fascinating commentary on the General Confession.

Screwtape Letters. C. S. LEWIS. Centenary Press. 5/-.

A penetrating understanding of the good and evil in human nature.

THE FACT OF JUDGMENT (page 28)

God's Judgment on Europe. ALEC R. VIDLER. Longmans. 4/-.

A valuable commentary on the present situation.

The Wrath and Peace of God. STEPHEN NEILL. Christian Literates Society for India. 2/-.

A very able treatment of certain fundamental doctrines of the Faith set forth in the Epistle to the Romans.

THE WORK OF REDEMPTION (page 29)

The Doctrine of our Redemption. N. MICKLEM. Eyre & Spottiswoode. 4/6.

A very satisfactory study of the Cross in Christian history.

Forgiveness and Reconciliation. VINCENT TAYLOR. Macmillan. 10/-.

A masterly treatise by a great authority on Biblical doctrine.

The Mediator. EMIL BRUNNER. Lutterworth Press. 25/-.

A great work on the central doctrine of the Christian faith, by a well-known champion of Barthian views.

CHAPTER III

THE APOSTOLATE OF THE WHOLE CHURCH

Evangelism. Tambaram Madras Series, Vol. III. O.U.P.
> It has good preliminary chapters on evangelism in general.

The Obedience of a Christian Man. E. P. DICKIE. S.C.M. 6/-.
> A book on the Christian doctrine of man and its implications.

Winning Men for Christ. Various authors. From C. G. Bridge.
30 Brompton Square, S.W. 3.
> A book full of useful and revealing data.

PRAYER (page 45)

I.   ELEMENTARY

The School of Prayer. OLIVE WYON. S.C.M. 6/-.
> An exceedingly able little book with illustrations gathered from the saints from almost every church in every age.

Prayer for All Christians. BEDE FROST. Mowbrays. 2/6.
> A simple and straightforward introduction to prayer.

When Ye Pray. BERNARD CLEMENTS. S.C.M. 2/6.
> A good introduction for the average Christian.

The Groundwork of Prayer. R. LUMB. Faith Press. 4/-.
> A very good book designed for the guidance and help of both preachers and teachers.

Training in Prayer. LINDSAY DEWAR. Rich & Cowan. 3/6.
> Another useful book of a practical kind.

Priesthood and Prayer. BEDE FROST. Mowbrays. 3/6.
> An extremely useful book for all clergy.

2.   MORE ADVANCED

Prayer. FREDERICK HEILER. O.U.P. 6/-.
> A standard work on prayer, tracing its rise and development through the ages.

Prayer and the Service of God. DANIEL JENKINS. Faber & Faber. 5/-.
> A book that treats the subject of prayer from a new standpoint. Contains an exceptionally clear diagnosis of the ills of modern society, written from a very definite theological point of view.

Abba. EVELYN UNDERHILL. Longmans. 2/6.
> A treatment of prayer based on the Lord's Prayer.

Creative Prayer. E. HERMAN. J. Clark & Co.
> An indispensable and helpful book.

N.B.—The following belong to the category of classical works on prayer:

Introduction to a Devout Life. FRANCIS DE SALES.

Spiritual Exercises. ST. IGNATIUS (arranged by Longridge).

Letters to Men and *Letters to Women.* ARCHBISHOP FENELON.

KNOWLEDGE OF THE BIBLE (page 46)

The Miracle Stories of the Gospels. A. RICHARDSON. S.C.M. 6/-.

The latest treatment of the subject ably written from a conservative standpoint.

The Bible View of Life. S. C. CARPENTER. Eyre & Spottiswoode. 7/6.

A book that shows very clearly the bearing of the Bible on the problems of ordinary life.

Preface to Bible Study. ALAN RICHARDSON. S.C.M. 6/-.

An important book written for those who want to know more about what the Bible teaches than about criticism and similar matters.

The Teaching of the Bible. BEDE FROST. Mowbrays. 5/-.

A new book written with a special purpose of helping teachers of all kinds to impart what the Bible teaches about essential Christian truths.

The Authority of the Bible. C. H. DODD. Nisbet. 12/6.

An authoritative book on the subject.

Supreme Encounter. BASIL MATTHEWS. S.C.M. 6/-.

A very readable book on the relevance of the Bible to the problems of to-day, with special reference to society and politics.

The Throne of David. A. G. HEBERT. Faber & Faber. 12/6.

The main theme of this book is to explain why the Old Testament forms an integral and essential part of the Bible, and deals with a number of outstanding theological ideas.

UNDERSTANDING OF HUMAN PERSONALITY (page 46)

Some Principles of Moral Theology. K. E. KIRK. Longmans. 16/-.

A masterly treatise on the outstanding problems connected with the spiritual life.

THE ART OF PREACHING (page 46)

The Servant of the Word. H. H. FARMER. Nisbet. 6/6.

The latest and one of the best books on preaching.

The Preacher's Theme To-day. WILLIAM TEMPLE. MacMillan. 4/6.

Deals with the two main themes, the nature and task of the Christian Church and Christian theology and modern thought.

THE CONDUCT OF DISCUSSION GROUPS (page 47)

The Padre's Hour. J. E. JESSOP. C.C.M.F. 6d.

Only a pamphlet, but extremely valuable.

Christian Faith in Action. J. E. JESSOP. 4 pamphlets. 6d. each. C.C.M.F.

Four extremely valuable little books designed primarily for the use of Chaplains, but equally useful for the preacher and the teacher. They are brilliantly written by one who has keen insight into both the nature and the demands of the Faith.

EVANGELISM IN THE HOME (page 58)

Home and Family Life. Report. S.C.M. 1/-.

A report by the British Council of Churches.

Home, Community and Church. Report. S.C.M. 1/-.

A report by a Church of Scotland Commission.

Thy Children shall be Taught. MARJORIE WRIGHT. Mowbrays. 2/-.

An excellent and helpful book for mothers.

Prayers for Expectant Mothers. S.P.C.K. 1/-.

Excellent preparation for motherhood.

EVANGELISM IN THE WORKING WORLD (page 60)

Social Witness and Evangelism. WILLIAM TEMPLE. Epworth Press. 2/6.

This forms a kind of sequel to Dr. Temple's Penguin volume (see Chapter I, General) and contains a very valuable appendix on evangelism in the modern world.

The Idea of Christian Society. T. S. ELIOT. Faber & Faber. 5/-.

An enquiry into what really constitutes a "Christian Society" in comparison with the present condition of affairs in so-called "Christian" England.

Christianity, Politics and Power. GERHARD LEIBHOLZ. C.N-L. Sheldon Press. 1/6.

Lectures originally delivered in Oxford. A really first-rate study of the subject. Recommended by Professor Hodgson.

Biblical Politics. ALEXANDER MILLER. S.C.M. 2/6.

Clear and concise studies in Christian social doctrine by a member of the Iona Community.

God, Man and Society. V. R. DEMANT. S.C.M. 2/6.

The sub-title, "An Introduction to Christian Sociology," aptly describes its contents. A very thorough treatment of the whole subject.

Christianity and Social Order. WILLIAM TEMPLE. Penguin. 9d.

A first-rate treatment of the social problem.

Christ the Lord of All Life. I.C.F. 1/6.

A very useful handbook covering all the great essential doctrines of the Christian Faith, with special reference to the problems presented by modern life.

CHAPTER IV

EVANGELISM. PROCLAIMING THE GOSPEL

THE EXPANSION OF CHRISTIANITY WITHIN SOCIETY (page 69)

Christianity in Thought and Practice. WILLIAM TEMPLE. S.C.M. 2/6.
   A short but very satisfactory treatment of theology and ethics.

Christian Faith and Life. WILLIAM TEMPLE. S.C.M. 3/-.
   A brief edition of the main themes set out in Christus Veritas.

The Relevance of Christianity. F. R. BARRY. Nisbet. 12/6.
   A book which first examines the teaching of Christ in considerable fullness
   and then systematically applies it to the various aspects of common life.

Christian Faith and the Common Life. Various authors. Allen & Unwin.
   7/6.
   Contains articles by such writers as W. Temple, R. Niebuhr, H. H. Farmer.

PAROCHIAL MISSIONS (page 74)

Parochial Missions. PETER GREEN.
   A useful handbook.

Our Fellowship in the Gospel. PATRICK C. A. CARNEGY. S.P.C.K.
   2/6.
   A very good handbook on evangelism, stressing the essential elements of
   the Gospel to be presented.

Go . . . Ye Teach : The Parochial Convention explained. CHARLES
   LAMBERT. S.P.C.K. 2/6.
   The sub-title explains the scope of this useful little book.

EVANGELISM AMONG CHILDREN (page 87)

Books suitable for children are constantly appearing, and reference
should be made to *The Focus Book Corner (S.P.C.K.), The Children's
Special Service Mission, The National Society, The Mothers' Union.*

In conjunction with them special recommendation is made of *New Testament Wall Pictures. E. A. Wood. S.P.C.K. 6d. each.*

The Life of Jesus of Nazareth. Illustrated by W. Hole. Eyre & Spottiswoode.
   Nothing better has yet been produced.

The Children's Book of Hymns. Blackie & Sons.
   The best collection of children's hymns.

Good and Gay. MARY OSBORNE. S.P.C.K. 2/6.
A picture book of prayer and praise.

The Children's Kingdom. GWENDOLINE WATTS. Oxford Blackwell.
Another book of praise and prayer.

A Thanksgiving for Children. MARGARET TEMPEST. Collins. 2/6.
Especially useful for small children.

If Jesus came to My House.

A stands for Angel. } JOAN GALE THOMAS. Mowbrays. 2/6.

Our Father.

These are undoubtedly to be placed among some of the best books for children in existence.

A Child's Guide to Morning Prayer. MARGARET CHESTER. S.P.C.K. 6d.

Little Christians' Pilgrimage and Christiana. HELEN TAYLOR. Well Gardner. 3/6.
The best children's edition of the Pilgrim's Progress.

EVANGELISM AND YOUTH (page 92)

The Approach to Religion in the Club. N.A.G.C. & M.C. 1/-.
Methods of approach along the lines of the interests of the members.

Religion in Boys' Clubs. N.A.B.C. 9d.
The report of an important Commission. It insists that "spiritual well-being" needs the sure foundation of a religious faith.

Girls Growing Up. A. P. JEPHCOTT. Faber & Faber. 6/-.
A penetrating and disturbing analysis.

Clubs for Girls. PEARL JEPHCOTT. Faber & Faber. 2/6.
An invaluable introduction.

Programme Possibilities for Church Youth Groups. S.C.M. 1/-.
A handbook of programme suggestions along the lines of Worship, Bible Study, Doctrine, Church History, Christian Responsibility and Evangelism.

Christian Leadership in the Service of Youth. S.C.M. 6d.
A statement prepared by the Youth Department of the British Council of Churches and commended by the late Archbishop of Canterbury as offering "wisdom and inspiration for a specially important and singularly difficult enterprise."

Christian Youth Work and the Future. British Council of Churches. 6d.
A consideration of the prospects for Christian youth work opened up by new educational legislation.

Club Leadership. BASIL L. Q. HENRIQUES. Oxford University Press. 5/-.

A standard text-book on boys' clubs.

The Teachers' Commentary. E. H. MARTIN. S.C.M. 7/6.

Helps to the Study of the Bible. O.U.P. 5/-.

Contains a concordance, many O.T. illustrations, and maps.

Dogma and Youth Work. G. W. O. ADDLESHAW. Dacre Press. 6d.

ECUMENICAL CO-OPERATION (page 96)

Revelation and Reunion. G. W. BLOOMFIELD. S.P.C.K. 7/6.

A really profound effort to re-examine the fundamental principles of religion in an attempt to discover a new basis for co-operation and unity.

Unity in the Truth. A. G. HEBERT. S.P.C.K. 2/6.

An examination of an outline of a reunion scheme from an Anglo-Catholic point of view.

The Nature of Catholicity. D. T. JENKINS. Faber & Faber. 5/-.

A really brilliant and original discussion on the subject of reunion by a Non-Conformist who has been greatly influenced by such diverse elements as Barthian theology, Sir Edwin Hoskyns and Father Hebert.

Christian Reunion. HUGH MARTIN. S.C.M. 6/-.

A survey of the problem with a plea for action from the Free Church point of view.

The Gospel in the Catholic Church. A. M. RAMSEY. Longmans. 7/6.

This book has a definite theological purpose, which is to assist the reunion movement.

CHAPTER VI

THE CHURCH, CHRIST'S WEAPON FOR EVANGELISM

Preface to Christian Theology. J. A. MACKAY. Nisbet. 7/6.

An absolutely invaluable introduction to the problems of theology in the modern world.

The Relevance of the Church. F. R. BARRY. Nisbet. 7/6.

An indispensable work for the study of the Church and its life at the present time. A sequel to his *Relevance to Christianity.*

Doctrine in the Church of England. The Report of the Commission on Christian Doctrine. S.P.C.K. 4/-.

Doctrines of the Creed. O. C. QUICK. Nisbet. 12/6.

A very satisfactory treatment of the great doctrines of the Christian Church. Perhaps Dr. Quick's greatest work.

Then and Now. JOHN FOSTER. S.C.M. 6/-.

A fascinating study of Church history in which modern conditions are compared with earlier ages.

What is the Church Doing ? H. P. VAN DUSEN. S.C.M. 6/-.

A stimulating work describing the activities of the Church in the present emergency.

World Church. JOHN FOSTER. S.C.M. 6/-.

Another study of Church history by the author of "Then and Now."

THE FELLOWSHIP OF THE CHURCH (page 122)

The Common Life in the Body of Christ. L. S. THORNTON. Dacre Press. 30/-.

A very valuable study of the Koinonia in the N.T. This book is almost a N.T. theological commentary in itself.

The Church and its Function in Society. W. A. VISSER 'T HOOFT and J. H. OLDHAM. Allen & Unwin. 8/6.

A very valuable and lucid study of the Church in modern society.

The Form of the Church. A. G. HEBERT. Faber. 8/6.

An endeavour by a well-known Anglo-Catholic to distinguish between the essential forms of the Church such as the ministries, creeds, etc., and the secondary forms, such as liturgies.

THE TRAINING OF THE CHURCH IN THE FAITH (page 127)

The Church and its Teaching To-day. WILLIAM TEMPLE. Macmillan. 4/6.

Deals with the two main themes, the nature and task of the Christian Church and Christian theology and modern thought.

The Christian Cell and its Place in the Church. Report. S.P.C.K. 1/-.
A very useful description of this particular movement.

Creed or Common Sense. SIR CHARLES JEFFRIES. Faber & Faber. 5/-.
A splendid book for the layman.

Jesus Christ the Teacher. W. A. CURTIS. O.U.P. 10/-.
A splendid study for lay people and students.

The Priest as Student. Various writers. S.P.C.K. 8/6.
An extremely good book by a number of experts. At the end of each chapter there is a very full bibliography.

The Catechism in Action. Various writers. Church Teaching Fellowship. 2/-.
A series of able addresses on the problems of Church teaching centring principally in the Catechism.

You. BEDE FROST. Mowbrays. 3/6.
A description of our human nature from the Christian standpoint for all ages. An introduction for Christian teachers.

The Household of Faith. S. C. CARPENTER, and a Chaplain. Nisbet. 3/-.
A new book specially designed to assist Church people in vindicating their faith and their Church before the world.

Beyond Personality. C. S. LEWIS. Centenary Press. 2/6.
Extraordinarily sane lectures on certain aspects of Christian doctrine, exposing several current fallacies and heresies.

THE WORSHIP OF THE CHRISTIAN CHURCH (page 134)

Worship. EVELYN UNDERHILL. Nisbet. 12/6.
A great book and a standard work on the subject.

The Vision of God. K. E. KIRK. Longmans. 7/6.
An abridgment of Dr. Kirk's Bampton Lectures dealing largely with the ethical significance of worship.

Liturgy and Society. A. G. HEBERT. Faber & Faber. 8/6.
An essay on the Church and her message as embodied in the order of the Church and her liturgy in the relation to the problem of belief and a true social life.

The Christian Sacraments. O. C. QUICK. Nisbet. 12/6.
A well-known and outstanding book on the subject.

Living Worship. E. G. PECK. Eyre & Spottiswoode. 4/6.
Quite a useful but rather difficult book on this important subject.

The Necessity of Worship. P. McLAUGHLIN. Dacre Press. 1/6.

A small but very valuable treatment on the whole subject of liturgy and worship.

Training in Worship. LINDSAY DEWAR and PHYLLIS DENT. Rich and Cowan. 5/-.

A very useful handbook for all engaged in parochial life.

Church Worship and the Non-Churchgoer. G. W. IRESON. S.P.C.K. 2/6.

This book deals with the difficult subject of youth and worship, facing the problems and suggesting solutions.

The Shape of the Liturgy. DOM GREGORY DIX. Dacre Press. 45/-.

A really great work on the form and development of the Liturgy by a recognised authority to which no mere summary can attempt to do justice.

Printed and made in Great Britain by
PARRETT & NEVES, LTD.
Rochester, Chatham and Gillingham